THE OCHRE BORDER

THE OCHRE BORDER

A JOURNEY THROUGH THE TIBETAN FRONTIERLANDS

JUSTINE HARDY

CONSTABLE · LONDON

First published in Great Britain 1995
by Constable and Company Limited
3 The Lanchesters, 162 Fulham Palace Road
London W6 9ER
Copyright © Justine Hardy 1995
ISBN 0 09 474090 9
The right of Justine Hardy to be
identified as the author of this work
has been asserted by her in accordance with
the Copyright, Designs and Patents Act 1988
Set in Linotron Ehrhardt 10pt by
Rowland Phototypesetting Ltd
Bury St Edmunds, Suffolk
Printed in Great Britain by
St Edmundsbury Press Ltd
Bury St Edmunds, Suffolk

A CIP catalogue record for this book
is available from the British Library

FOR SARAH
because she wanted to go
but never had the chance

CONTENTS

ILLUSTRATIONS

(Photographs by Will Curtis)

ACKNOWLEDGEMENTS

This book is an attempt to capture a verbal snapshot of a place that will change in the same way that scenes from our childhood differ when revisited later in life. That initial memory is the one that we cling to. This is about a people and a place cocooned by 70 years of isolation from the outside world before the inevitable bolt toward the 21st century. The Spiti Valley will alter and it would be naive to think that it could remain as we found it in September 1992. We were lucky to get in when we did and for this I would like to thank a few people: Roma Satara, Paddy Singh and Reggie Singh for opening all the doors that initially closed in my face; Maggie Noach and Constable Publishers for taking a punt on me, Peter Hopkirk for his support and advice and Willy Dalrymple for saying encouraging things about me to the right people. I owe Christian a great deal for his patience, my mother and father for letting me run away and Will for all the snaps. If there are aspects that offend my fellow travellers then I hope they will understand that I have just tried to give a portrayal of what we found. I must apologise to Jane Northway because her name has been changed to Ella in the text to avoid the confusion of there being two Janes. The main debt is to the people of Spiti who let us in.

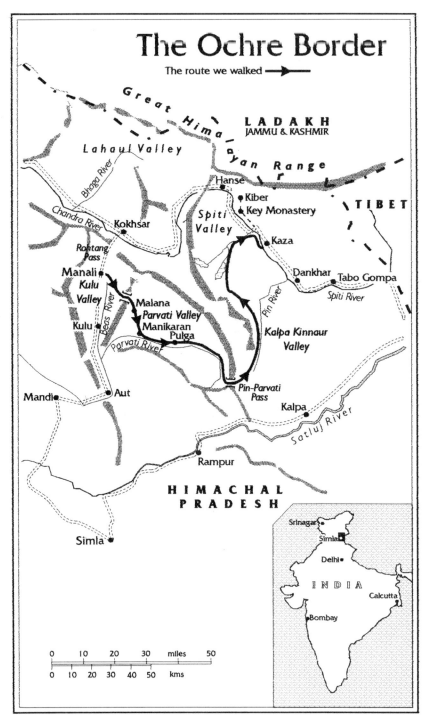

The Ochre Border

The route we walked ⟶

Great Himalayan Range

LADAKH
JAMMU & KASHMIR

Lahaul Valley

Bhaga River

Hanse

Kiber

Key Monastery

TIBET

Chandra River

Kokhsar

Spiti Valley

Kaza

Rohtang Pass

Dankhar

Tabo Gompa

Manali

Kulu Valley

Malana

Parvati Valley

Manikaran

Pulga

Spiti River

Kulu

Beas River

Parvati River

Kalpa Kinnaur Valley

Pin River

Mandi

Aut

Pin-Parvati Pass

Kalpa

Satluj River

Rampur

HIMACHAL PRADESH

Simla

Srinagar

Simla

Delhi

INDIA

Calcutta

Bombay

| 0 | 10 | 20 | 30 | miles | 50 |

| 0 | 10 | 20 | 30 | 40 | 50 | kms |

INTRODUCTION

A small boy with a shaven head picks himself up out of the dust. His puppy-wrestling companion flicks his robe over his shoulder and walks away, the stubble on his head picked out by the early morning light. The boy shakes like a dog; a cloud of dust comes from his ochre robes. He sets off with a crab-like gait but, as he walks, he straightens and becomes older. He approaches a stranger standing in the corner of the monastery courtyard.

'Do you read the books of Julian Barnes?' asks the eight-year-old Buddhist novice.

This is a scene from the Spiti Valley on the Indo-Tibetan Border. If you look at an atlas it is on the dotted line between the pink of India and the yellow spread of China; part of the border area that does not appear to belong to anyone. It is a last untainted pocket where the past runs up against the future.

India cheered Independence in 1947 and two years later Mao Tse-tung announced The People's Republic of China. For a pregnant moment the two nations embraced each other; the new juvenile leads that had escaped from the wicked stepmother of ruling oppression. The pantomime ended in 1949 when Peking Radio and the official New China News Agency announced that 'Tibet as well as Turkestan are integral parts of China,' and 'the British and American imperialists and their stooge, the Indian Nehru government,' ran the risk of 'cracking their skulls against the mailed fist of the great Chinese People's Liberation Army' if they gave their support to Tibet. The following October the 'mailed fist' massed on the Eastern Border and invaded Tibet. The Tibetans crumpled in the Chinese sweep across their country. The cultural and physical pillage and torture that followed are still an unfolding twentieth century horror story.

But, in the high reaches of the Himalayas, near the Indian Border, satellites of Tibet survived intact. They are known as the disputed border area and waved the Indian flag at the Chinese to shout their impunity. They shut their borders and waited for the danger to recede.

In 1977 small parts of these areas were opened up with a certain amount of big brother watchfulness. Permits were limited. They were often ignored by recalcitrant border police who wielded their permit stamps like AK47s.

In 1992 the Spiti and Lahaul Valleys once more opened their borders to a few visitors. For those who managed to wheedle past the jumpy border guards the reward was to find an area of The High Himalayas that has managed to preserve itself as a severed limb of Tibet; an anachronism of Tantric Buddhism and medieval farming methods.

The people weave their lives around a labyrinth of demons, saints and holy men. Their religious rituals shroud themselves in the same sort of mystic diversity that spreads from the intensity of the Catholic Communion to the merry extreme of hanky waving Morris Dancers.

Their Buddhism runs parallel with their daily lives. The shrines in their homes are splattered with cooking fat and they will recite a *mantra* (sacred phrase) in the same breath as they yell at their yaks.

Theirs is a disappearing world that is being chipped at from the outside. As the borders open the travellers will begin to filter in. With each click of the visitors' camera shutters the mountain people get a bit wiser to the fast buck potential of tourism.

When we walked in they were villagers in high places raised on a diet of barley flour and Buddhism. What does that make them? Neither gods nor strange inbreeds. They are a high altitude people with raisin skin and a wicked sense of humour. They use wooden ploughs pulled by yaks; they hum mantras in the same way that we burble advertising jingles; they feed their dead to the birds; they gallop on tiny ponies across mountain rubble and they believe in primogeniture.

Few people have seen these valleys. More will, but at the risk of losing the bloom off the fruit. To each visitor it will mean something else; an area with a chameleon aspect. Rudyard Kipling described a scene in *Kim* when the young man and the old lama reach the Chinni Valley. On a map the valleys are many days climb apart but the description could have been Spiti:

'At last they entered a different world within a world – a valley of leagues where the high hills were fashioned of the mere rubble and refuse from the knees of the mountains ... surely the gods live here, beaten down by the silence and the appalling sweep of the dispersal of the cloud shadows after rain. This place is no place for man.'

So I decided to go.

[1]

A LOST VALLEY

T HE priest had bare feet; dark, well-worn bare feet and they were right under my nose. It is not that easy to take Communion in the right frame of mind when faced at the holy rail by a pair of naked brown feet, peering at you from beneath a cassock. The choir was trickling into a saccharin hymn about children and flowers. The man on the left at the rail had been given such a short back and sides that his scalp showed through the close crop. The buttons on his blazer were so highly polished that they reflected his nasal hairs.

The notices had been about a coffee morning to raise money for the state leprosy hospital. Apart from the predominance of saris and the talk of leprosy it could have been another Sunday morning in any English county town. But this was Simla, the state capital of Himachal Pradesh.

This was where I first heard about the lost valleys of the High Himalayas.

Simla has wrapped itself up in the past. It was the summer capital of the Raj when the heat in the plains started to addle their minds. They built bungalows like those around the golf courses of turn of the century Surrey. They called their houses names such as Rose Cottage and Wood-lands. They planted herbaceous borders and standard roses in the gardens. They filled their days with gymkhanas, picnics, cocktail parties and sexual intrigue. The town now echoes with the ghosts of the Viceroy's entourage, kept alive by the old Indian families who still mourn the departure of 'The Britishers'.

We were having tea in the courtyard. There was a linen tablecloth and Limoges tea cups. There were crumpets with dark yellow butter. My host was Reggie, Kanwar of Karpurthala, the title given to the younger brother of a maharajah. The other tea drinker was Captain Padam Singh, a lolloping Indian who speaks English more comfortably than his own language. His fame precedes him and he is known by most people north of Delhi. His past has an air of colourful intrigue. He is known to many wise travellers and pretty girls simply as Paddy. His ambling six foot four figure is familiar to most English people who have ever spent any time in North India. Reggie and he were harking back to their youth in the army while I watched the butter melt through the holes in my crumpet.

'I went into Spiti in 1963 on manoeuvres. I am telling you it was the most god awful place. To be getting there we had to drag ourselves over some of the worst passes I have ever been over. We had no proper maps, no one knew anything about the place. All we had was a 1945 US Airforce map. It was about as much use as a virgin in a brothel. When we got there what did we find? Nothing, absolutely nothing. Just empty valleys and villages full of simple people.' Paddy waved his long arms expansively.

I asked him what he meant by empty valleys and simple people.

'*Achchhà* (every Indian's favourite exclamation roughly translated as 'Oh' or 'OK') I mean nothing; just nothing, so much nothing that you can hear the porter half a mile behind you breathing,' he replied.

'Really Paddy?' I asked.

'You don't know how loudly you will be breathing when you get to 17 000 feet. I sounded like someone shaking a box of dried peas and I didn't have TB, but the porter did.' Paddy laughed.

'When you say nothing do you mean that there is no landscape?' I said.

'Yes, yes, the landscape is very big. They call it the Valley of the Gods. But all the valleys are called Valley of the Gods. We are just lucky that we have enough gods to fill them all.'

'What about the people?' I asked.

'What do you think people who have always lived up in the mountains would be like? They have not seen any outsider really for about seventy years. How old is your father?'

'I'm not sure. I think he is sixty-five,' I replied.

'Most of the villagers have not seen an outsider for five years longer than your father has been alive; nearly a full lifetime.' Paddy looked mysterious.

'Can you get in?' I was already beginning to plan.

'No. I only got in because I was on manoeuvres with the army.'

'Oh.' End of the planning.

'They are going to allow some people in next year. I know the people. I can get you a permit. I will show them your work. It will be no problem.' He smiled right to his back teeth.

'Paddy, when you say "no problem" that is just when the problems start.' I know Paddy well enough to know when to be wary.

'I am very serious. The passes are open from July until September. It is the wet time in July and August so the best time would be September.' Paddy ate another crumpet; his way of completing the deal.

Tea and crumpets in the freeze-dried Raj setting seemed too far away from snow fields on the Tibetan border to treat the idea as anything more than teatime conversation.

Nine months later the wheels were rumbling into motion and I was in Stanfords Maps and Charts shop in Covent Garden looking for a map to find my way around Spiti.

I asked the assistant if they had any maps of the disputed border region of Indian Tibet above Nepal. She laughed when I told her that the last map that I had come across of the area was a 1945 US Airforce map.

'I'm sure that we can do better than that,' she told me confidently as she began to rummage through shelves of maps.

I left Stanfords armed with a 1945 US Airforce map.

I went digging in the library to see what I could find. The librarian asked me when I was thinking of going to Yugoslavia. She told me that she and her boyfriend had had such a fine time on one of the islands there.

I looked at her, rather surprised.

'I don't think I'm going to Yugoslavia, am I?' I was trying to work out what she was talking about.

'Spiti is in Yugoslavia, isn't it?' she asked.

As I dug deeper the area seemed to become more remote as only snippets of information came to light.

The reception to my idea at home was what I had expected. This was going to be my fifth 'great trip' into the Himalayas. Each time the novelty wore off a little more until the family began to look on me as someone who needed an annual fix of India.

My mother immediately had a vision of her daughter sprawled on a mountainside, cut off from civilization and half dead.

'How wonderful,' she said when I told her but she did not really look as if she believed it. 'You will be taking a man with you, won't you darling? You will have William with you like the last time, won't you? He knows what to do, doesn't he?' She has travelled to most parts of the earth so her advice is not usually the fretting of a xenophobic mother figure.

My father was resigned.

'Ah, you're going back to India again. Where are you going to this time? Is there any of it that you haven't seen?' he asked.

'Yes. The Tibetan border area. No outsider has really been in since the Chinese invaded Tibet in the 50's. It is a small box that the old Tibet has been shut up in and protected by,' I babbled, trying to enthuse him with the idea of this adventure.

'Oh God, I suppose you will get shot at by the Chinese,' he intoned.

'I don't think so, the Chinese did not really get that far,' I said.

'Just remember that they have a medieval attitude towards life. You are not somebody's daughter to them. You are just another body for them to put a bullet or a knife into if the mood takes them.' He had his back to me so I could not tell how serious his expression was.

Friends regarded my idea as another step on the inevitable ladder towards insanity, and a traveller's graveyard.

'Where did you say you were going?' one of them asked in an unguarded moment. I started the story about the Chinese and the last protected remnant of Tibet but the listener had switched off.

'That's nice. Will you be back in time for our wedding or am I going to have to send your invitation to some ridiculous poste restante shack in the middle of nowhere? And please, nothing too beardy weirdy for a wedding present.'

They had a point. Once you have been labelled as a traveller it is difficult for people to keep up with you, or to remember where you have been. It is all very well going off to rediscover the diminishing tribes of the High Himalayas, but it is not everyone's idea of a gripping tale.

Others took more of an interest.

'You are going to wake up one morning and your backpack will have become another part of your anatomy,' said another friend.

'I won't take a backpack,' I replied.

'Why not?'

'Because I would have to carry it.' I was not a good advertisement for pushing out the frontiers of travel.

'What do you use then?' He was becoming irritated.

'A suitcase.'

'You mean you carry a suitcase over the Himalayas?' He was now irritated and intrigued.

'No,' I said.

'Who carries your stuff then?' he asked.

'A porter.'

'But I thought you were a real traveller,' he accused.

'If I was a real traveller I would be sitting on a dusty platform in the lotus position, waiting for a train that is never going to come, to take me to somewhere no one has ever been.' I could hear how smug I sounded.

'So you're a fake?'

'If you put it like that, yes, I suppose I am.' I could not really argue with that.

'I suppose you are going to take a helicopter into this wonderful new place as the train is never going to get you there.' He was on the attack now.

'No, I'm going to walk there.'

'What do you mean walk?' he asked.

'Hannibal managed the Alps with elephants; I think I can make it across a rather small section of the Himalayas with my suitcase,' I replied.

There were bigger stumbling blocks to face than justifying the journey to friends and family. The Indian authorities would only give permits to groups of five people or more. So far there was just the photographer Will, and me.

So began a rapid assault on the Buddhist Centres of London. There were meetings with shaven-headed, Western Buddhists, their white hairy legs sticking out from under their ochre and orange robes. They all have exotic Buddhist names that must give them a great deal more mysticism than trying to meditate as just plain Graham or Sue. They all loved the idea of entering into this cupping bowl of Tibetan learning, but when it came down to the screws and widgets of having to buy plane tickets and walk up mountains, their enthusiasm dwindled.

I began an advertising campaign.

'Oh, you find that your priorities all fall into place. The annoying man in front of you in the supermarket queue who forgot to weigh his vegetables, is a lifetime away. The mountains and the people are like a huge concentrate of all the good intentions that you have ever had,' I found myself saying to people.

I made posters about the trip and put them in what I thought would be suitable places.

The one at Pineapple Dance Centre in South Kensington brought in a flood of replies from fitness fanatics who saw it as the ultimate diet and get fit regime. I discovered a hundred ways of saying no to the fitness set. Most of them were put off by the idea of wallowing in their own filth without a bath in sight for weeks on end.

The French Language School seemed to be a more genuine field of potential. Three very pretty girls were enthusiastic about going. I had to

gently discourage them when my stumbling French grappled a fundamental fact. They were more interested in discovering Tantric sex than
donning a pair of trekking boots to set forth to new lands.

Time was beginning to run out.

A Norwegian girl said it was her life's dream to go to Tibet and she
signed on the dotted line. Hopping up mountains seemed to have been
her family's thing. Her English was not good and there was going to be
a certain amount of groundwork when it came to a sense of humour. On
the positive side she had been to Nepal twice and she had a good grasp
of Buddhism: she was the girl for the trip. Then her father had a heart
attack and she fled to Oslo, so it was back to square one.

At last I found an itinerant school friend looking for a voyage of discovery. Jane was between the devil and the deep blue sea of two years of
dusty bliss in the Australian Outback, and a recent return to the social
strictures of South-west London. Ah . . . India, the panacea for Western
broken hearts and U-turn career paths.

The eleventh hour was ticking into sight when two girls who had seen
a poster at their local Buddhist Centre called. I was so desperate that they
should come that I tried the tack of nonchalance; the other worldliness
of a hardened traveller. It did not last long before I was drowning them
in high altitude rhetoric.

Both of them wanted and needed a break.

Amanda had just sold her pre-prep school and was missing her babes.
She needed something to fill the vacuum that had appeared where she
had once wielded her teaching power. Ella, because her life read more
like a Jay McInerney novel than the real thing. Somebody, somewhere
owed her something in return for all the hard luck stories she had.

Now we were five; four girls and Will. I did not draw his attention to
the fact that he was setting off as the only man on the mountain. Once
we were there, the porters would put the girls into a minority.

The run-up to departure became governed by lists. Lists of things to
take, lists of things not to take, lists of jabs to have, lists of our lives, loves
and inside leg measurements for general perusal in various immigration
and visa departments. Whenever we met up we exchanged pieces of paper
like religious relics that were poured over and inwardly digested then
immediately forgotten. We waved them at people in shops, and at the visa
departments like white flags.

The final hitches came with the confirmation of our airline tickets. I
got quite good at flirting with airline officials. On the back of this there
were ridiculous conversations with Paddy and an intrusive third party

who always seemed to be doing their tumble drying on the long distance connection.

Paddy: 'You know (tumble, tumble wrrr) when you want to come?'

'What did you say?'

Paddy: 'I am telling you it has been (rumble wrrr rumble) for a month now.'

'What has it been doing?'

Paddy: '(wrrr rumble) . . . ning ning.'

'Not raining?'

Paddy: 'It will have rained itself out soon.'

'How soon?'

Paddy: 'What are we now, yes June, it will have rained itself out by (wrrrrrr) . . . mber.'

'Was that September or November?'

Paddy: 'Oh my god no, not November, much too late then unless you want to go on an ice walk.'

'I think I'll leave that to Ranulph Fiennes.'

Paddy: 'No it is not fine, it must be earlier.'

We then lost the line completely and we were both left confused and short-tempered.

The new date was September and the girls were out buying trekking boots and ringing me up to tell me how many tonnes of traction they had on each sole. I was dismissive and said that I had crossed the Himalayas the year before in a pair of Reebok tennis shoes. Under cover of the sales, I did buy a pair of boots that went a long way to making me look like an extra in a chauvinist, lesbian film.

The next step was to try and tie up a commission with a magazine before we left the country. I returned from the meetings with no result and a standard reply from the travel editors.

'Well, no one has really heard of this place, have they?' was the first reaction I got.

'No, that's why I want to write about it,' I tried.

'I don't think we really want to take the risk of commissioning a piece about it until some more people know about the area. I think it is a bit remote at the moment,' said another from behind the brim of her travel editor's hat.

'But don't you want pieces that go away from the tequila slamming and the boutiques?' I asked.

'Yes, but we have to test the ground first. If it was up to me I would commission you here and now, but it is not that easy.' She smiled goodbye.

Each magazine office gave me a variation on this theme: great sounding place but no one has ever heard of it. This was not going to fill my bank account with pay cheques, but it did make our plan more unusual. If the travel editors had not heard of Spiti then we were perhaps less likely to bump into queues of other travel writers lining up to get into the last Shangri-La for their slice of the dream.

At last the travel permits arrived. We were off. There was a moment of panic when there were second thoughts, but we all went home to calmly pack our bags and file away our misgivings.

What did each of us think we were going to find?

We have no idea what we are going to find. We go because we get caught in a vortex of practicalities; each jab, each reference book, each till receipt is a step closer to take off. Then it is a journey, arriving, being there, and coming back. It is only afterwards, when we have shown all the photographs and embellished every anecdote, that we start to realise what we were looking for and what we actually found.

We often use travel as a placebo; if we run away, perhaps the problem will go away. Stumbling marriages hurry to tropical beaches in search of emotional glue; broken hearts cross deserts pitching physical endurance against mental scarring. It does not work.

How we see the places we travel to depends on what we are looking for. It is a bit like losing a contact lens. You spend hours spitting and hissing, combing across the carpet. Then someone will walk into the room, bend down and pick up your lens without even knowing that you had lost it.

The best portrayals of the faraway are often given by those who are not specialists on the country or its people. They have gone in without expecting too much and, like a sponge, they soak up what they find. They see their surroundings as if through a child's eye rather than with the critical appraisal of the professional traveller.

[2]

LANDING IN HIPPIE SOUP

DELHI stinks of life and death. It rushes at you when the doors of the airport open. The taxi wallahs dart in as you wave your prepaid voucher at them limply.

Donovan, our contact, was there waving, all neat and clean in pressed jeans and a bright white sweatshirt. It was four o'clock in the morning and even Ella's top knot, which had remained buoyant throughout the flight, had begun to head south.

Paddy could not meet us because he was stuck in the rain. There was a drought in Delhi, but Paddy had managed to find some rain to get stuck in on his way down from the mountains.

Indian Airlines were not sure if they would be able to fly us up to the Kulu Valley the following day as there had been too much rain.

The small plane did shudder out of Delhi Domestic Terminal the next morning and we arrived at Kulu airport intact.

Paddy was at the airport; all gangly six foot four of him, loping toward us across the tarmac.

'Welcome back to the Kulu Valley,' he beamed.

We had managed to make it to Manali in less than twenty-four hours from our arrival in Delhi. The distance does not look impressive on a map, but in terms of Indian bureaucracy and the temperament of the domestic airlines, it was an achievement.

Manali is the lentil-munching Mecca of India. A thousand bearded travel writers have set off from this town on their literary journey into the Himalayas.

It is a place where the West meets Himalayan mountain life in a hippie soup of pony tails, straggly beards, dhobi-frayed clothes, and 'the one that got away' travel tales. Everyone who has set forth on the hippie trail has a story to tell about Manali. Each year the cafés and 'very nice, very cheap' hotels spread a little further, chewing up the mountainside.

Ella and Amanda set out to buy ethnic in bulk to equip themselves for the trek. Will sighed a lot, shrugged at the leaden sky, and packed some silicate gel around his cameras. Jane became the first victim of bowel rebellion and was subjected to a barrage of useless advice. I tried out my rusty Hindi in the bazaar. In quieter moments I was quite proud of my vocabulary, gleaned over my years of to-ing and fro-ing from India. My pronunciation had the same effect as an Englishman shouting at a Parisian shopkeeper in schoolboy French. The bazaar stallholders wobbled their heads and I failed to get what I wanted. Most of them speak different mountain dialects and slow English had more effect than showing off in pidgin Hindi.

Thus thwarted in the bazaar, I set off in search of the mountain villages beyond Manali; the rural idylls that had inspired me to deep purple prose when I first came to the Kulu Valley.

In the courtyard of an old house a young man with white blonde hair and a Scandinavian travel tan was juggling brightly coloured balls. There was a gaggle of local children around him fascinated by his blue eyes and the spinning balls. One boy was trying to catch them as they dropped; jumping up to snatch at them before they flew up again. But they kept bouncing back up into the air, in a whirl of colour, just out of reach of his small, dark hands. From where I stood I could just hear their laughter above the sound of the builders and the digging trucks carving into the hillside next to this sweet, bright scene.

Old Manali is just across a narrow river from the main town, a few minutes walk, but a different world. The village is a jigsaw of wooden houses, where the cattle live on the ground floor, and pretty girls look out of carved casement windows onto the paths cobbled with dry cow dung. The villagers somehow manage to retain their clothes, customs and village hierarchy within spitting distance of the hotels and the digging trucks.

I scrambled up beyond the path, proud that my boots and I were being so brave. On the edge of the cliff I looked back down at my sheer ascent, smug and satisfied. The chatter of local girls came from behind a rock that looked as if it was balanced on thin air. They were bent double under piles of firewood and they had nothing more on their feet than thin plastic shoes; the Indian equivalent of those donned by sensible swimmers on the Cornwall Coast. They skipped down the route that I had just hauled myself up. I examined my tiny day pack containing just a midget camera, a compact tube of sun cream and a small bottle of water. Then I looked with humiliation at the huge bundles of firewood and set off after the firewood carriers. Within the first few strides I had tipped up, bounced down several rocks and stopped myself by grabbing a bush with sharp spikes; another lesson in mountain sense for the tourist who thinks that they can double as a goat.

The perennial backdrop to the bustle in Manali is the local Himachalis scuttling through the streets with their round hats and tweed coats. There are loud Kashmiris who come in to tout their trade out of the firing line in Srinagar. Many of the porters that hurry up and down the streets are Nepalese, hunched under their loads and hacking like old coalminers.

Even though Mr Bunsen was born and bred in Calcutta he is an important man in Manali. He is the bank manager at the State Bank of India. He gave us the thrill of skipping the long queue of travellers waving traveller's cheques at us with malice. India still seems to be a great example of 'it's not what you know, but who you know' and I know two of Mr Bunsen's most important clients. To complete the transaction we had to take tea with Mr Bunsen after the bank closed for the day.

We sat at Pete's Café, in the damp heat that follows Manali rain, looking out on a patch of sunflowers.

Once Pete's Café used to be Trish and Pete's Café. Pete found Trish, a happy hippie from the Welsh valleys, on a voyage of discovery in The Kulu. Indian Pete thought mixed racial relationships were cool and Trish came up with the idea of the café. It became the hot chocolate and *bhang lassi* haven of the hippie trail. Then Trish legged it and Pete and the café were left to limp on. There is still brown bread and an exhausted selection of quiches; but it has all become leaden without Trish's deft Welsh pastry hand. Pete has a faraway look in his eyes, probably the weed rather than unrequited love, and it takes half an hour to get a cup of chai.

When our round arrived the milk was floating on the top and the tea was tepid. Not quite the impression you want to make on your bank manager, but Mr Bunsen has been in Manali long enough to know that ordering coagulating chai is not necessarily a reflection of a person's collateral.

Mr Bunsen thought it was 'most very fantastic' that we were setting forth for the Spiti Valley. He gave his blessing to the venture and hoped that we would get there safely and 'pave the path for many peoples'. We could almost see the tourist figures spinning in his head.

What he was more interested in was whether Princess Diana really made herself throw up all the time and was Mr Morton really a friend of hers if he wrote all those things about her. He looked deep into his thickening chai, and voiced the opinion that it was most fortunate that the maharajahs had not been subjected to the same scrutiny as the Windsors or there would have been some most unsavoury cases. He started to murmur about young boys, unsuitable mistresses and the repulsive demise of a memsahib's toy dog. He thought better of his stories and the salacious mumbling was replaced by more cerebral matters.

We mused on various topics unrelated to the bank. If you have ever wondered what to do with those spiky courgettes that you see on the barrows of Westbourne Grove markets in Indian London, Mr Bunsen has a long and convoluted recipe that makes this strange, bitter vegetable almost edible. The main ingredients are to have a great deal of time and patience.

Paddy makes metaphorical curry with people. He chooses an odd mix and always expects something delicious to come out of it. As with all the best curries, the stranger the ingredients the more exciting the result. So we found ourselves as his curry, sitting on the floor of his house just outside Manali, drinking large glasses of mildly diluted whisky, and trying not to crumble fresh poppadums all over ourselves.

Paddy has had years of experience of drinking at high altitude but we had not. So we found ourselves discussing our deepest secrets with Glenys and Desireé, an Australian mother and daughter duet that Paddy had swept up off the streets of Manali. As the conversation became more absurd and profound Paddy tipped more IML into still full glasses to oil our thickening tongues. IML is Indian Manufactured Liquor; milder versions of the normal Western spirits but highly effective at anything over 10 000 feet. Paddy's elegant wife, Nita, did her best to soak up his liberal attitude with the whisky bottle by plying us with aubergine fritters, curry fried sweet potatoes and spicy *naan*. She was an angel of mercy through the alcoholic haze. The evening made the planned trip to the barber the next day seem a tricky task.

I have a friend in the back streets of Manali; a Tibetan barber. He is a walking advertisement for his trade as his head is always perfectly shaved in religious observation of mourning. He seems to have a great many cousins and aunts with a habit of dying as I have never seen him with anything but a clean shaven head.

His shop is a rickety chair in the street in front of a small table covered with the tools of his trade. There is a big old whisky bottle with a splash top filled with a strange eau de cologne, various sets of scissors, cut throat razors and several cracked and tarnished mirrors. He has a large, sagging umbrella over the rickety chair so that he can continue to ply his trade during the frequent Manali downpours. Beside the umbrella is a bench where his clients queue and are served small cups of scalding chai while they wait their turn in the rickety chair. The staff of Pete's Café should go and have a lesson in making chai from the stall next to the Tibetan barber.

Will and I had visited him on several earlier trips to Manali, both before and after treks, for a clean up and cut. Hair washing at 17 000 feet is a two minute recipe for a head cold. Some of the porters carry fleas and lice and there is nothing these mites like more than a luxuriant head of clean hair; the shorter and dirtier, the lower the chance of infestation.

Will had been shorn, and he was up and gone before I even managed to point my lens at him. I was at the front of the queue and into the chair. I showed the barber how much was to go, he grinned, and I closed my eyes. He sprayed, combed and cropped. Then he juggled my head in his hands and my neck groaned and crunched. The temple band was going past celebrating the festival of the Kulu Gods. It was a haphazard cacophony of cymbals, drums, horns and pipes. In a confined space it would have been terrifying. In the streets of Manali, after a 20p haircut and head massage, it was sweet music.

We returned to the orchard to attempt pruning our packing. Trying to fit every eventuality into a suitcase is impossible. When you head off to a place that is not even a dot on the map everything from typhoon wear to the need for white tie could crop up. All you really need are the clothes you are going to stand up in, day in day out, and one spare set for when the first set stand up and walk out on you, powered by their own stench. Try telling that to your brain when you are buried in your bag deciding what to take. Of course you need spare everything, right down to two copies of the medical section from the high altitude trekking guide, complete with gory details of what to expect when you take your last gasp with chronic altitude sickness. I like to think that I have mastered the art of capsule packing. There is a great deal of artistic licence with the size of the capsule.

If you ever do get the chance to set off on such an adventure bear the following in mind: take earplugs; it is surprising how penetrating snoring becomes in the mountain silence, and uninterrupted sleep is very important. Take a torch; it is more valuable than gold for girls with small bladders during long nights. The ultimate torch is the miner's lamp attached to your head, leaving your hands free for pyjamas, zips, books or food. Take sweets; the best ones are chocolate éclairs because the chocolate is insulated from dramatic melting by the outer shell. They become your succour at stressful times when hymn singing and logic fail. Carry a penknife with a sensible number of blades; the nail file and screwdriver blades are so versatile as to be the basis for 'Zen and The Art of Capsule Packing'. Find a flat, multi-fitting bath plug. I have been surprised by plugless basins in the most incongruous places. It is infuriating to miss a rare chance to wash due to the lack of a plug. Carry a love letter that you once read in a hurry. By the time you have read it a hundred times it has taken on a thousand meanings, become your lucky charm, and revitalised your love life. There is no need to list the obvious selection of garish and high tech mountain gear that you can mortgage your mother for. Every friend who has ever seen a mountain from a train window will give you endless advice about what to take. Just take as little as possible if you want to get to your goal and not run the gauntlet of tired porters going on strike at crucial moments.

Once we had managed to cut the weight of our packing down we met the men who were going to carry it all. We all have humbling moments in our lives. They usually come after a flash of pride. Ours came when we had sat smugly over our breakfast chapattis comparing the microscopic neatness of our packing. Then we met the porters. There were five of us, all young and fit; two small, one medium and two tall. There were twenty porters, all ages, all wiry; eighteen small and two tall by Nepalese standards. That was four porters each. That was humbling.

When faced with an army of porters it does not cross your mind that when there are that many of them, half of them are actually carrying food and equipment for themselves; in effect the porter's porters. You look at them and they look at you. You are the punters and they are the team.

These men are the breed that stamp around the parade squares of the British Military; highly polished and highly tuned. The Nepalese porters have the same physique but not quite the same attention to uniform as the Ghurkas. They are little power packs of knotted muscle with black darting eyes and pickled livers. Their strength in comparison to their height makes you reach for the iron pills. Medical journals tell us that each of our muscles has a breaking strain of a tonne and the porters seem set on testing this theory every day of their lives.

They stood in rows in front of us; a confusing crowd of mahogany faces. Most of them wore the customary loose tunics over cotton trousers. Some of them had done a bit of mix and match with articles of trekking wear, probably donated by previous grateful trekkers. A couple of them

[28]

looked about fourteen and there were others who could well have been grandfathers.

There seemed to have been a general command of 'eyes down' as twenty pairs took in our various models of brand new climbing boots. Nearly all of them were in the now familiar plastic beach shoes, with a couple in summery flip flops. My feet blushed in their monstrous boots.

Twenty Nepalese names do not trip off the tongue easily. They all ended with 'adur', so a mumbled first part and a strident 'adur' would be guaranteed to get a reaction from someone. By the time I had written down that Ranabadur wore a white jersey, and that Angrabadur had a moustache, every one of them seemed to have a white jersey and a moustache. I think it may also be a Nepalese habit to change your name as the mood suits you. None of us spoke Nepalese and their knowledge of Hindi and English was scant. There were not going to be expansive discussions over the camp fire. They were going to be carrying all our worldly goods, so we tried not to stare at their plastic shoes, and smiled at them enthusiastically. They laughed at us. They could afford to; we were in their hands.

Our two lead guides were familiar faces to Will and me as the Manali men whom Paddy retains. Sonam and Karma had led us over the Himalayas into Ladakh the previous year. Sonam's moon face had appeared at my tent every morning in a waft of tea and cardamom. 'Bed tea Memsahib' had been his daily call from Manali to Leh. Karma had become a hero in our eyes for his ability to make bread at 17 000 feet and for continuing to shave every day even when his face was pitted with blisters from the cold and the sun. The security of these old friends among the sea of porters caused a general round of hearty handshaking and reassurances of all our good health.

Our bags were packed up in sacking, in what now appeared to be mountainous piles, while the porters humped tents and gas stoves around. Paddy appeared in his truck.

We were finally about to leave in search of something that most people believe no longer exists; a place cushioned from the outside world for seventy years.

INTO THE MOUNTAINS

H EROINES are not supposed to be car sick, so I failed the audition early on.

Most initial travel planning seems to be on an elevated plane dealing with things that are frequently intangible; especially in the case of trying to get any kind of simple answer out of the Indian authorities. It is all too easy to fall into the hole of dealing with the theoretical rather than the practical. Henry V was so busy working out the penetration of his archers, and rallying his countrymen, that he did not think too much about the rain that was to bog down both armies and inflict screaming dysentery. In pursuit of a virgin land it had not crossed my mind that I might be attacked by the bogey man of motion sickness, or that we too, like Hank Cinq, would sink thigh deep into unexpected mud.

I was supposed to be the leader. Leaders do not go green and end up viewing the panorama of the Himalayas from the retching position. Leaders give their last rations to their fellow travellers and act as decoys in the face of marauding mountain men. They do not clutch their stomachs and wrestle with Stugeron packets. This limp leader did until we drove out of the Kulu Valley into the Parvati Valley.

The Kulu Valley has become a tourist and transit route. It is one of the corridors on the road to Leh. When the passes are open the roads have a constant traffic of Indian freight lorries. They are painted like fairground rides with curvaceous B Movie characters from the *Kama Sutra* idling on lotus leaves. The drivers' cabins are surrounded with tinsel and fairy lights, and the dashboards are a party of small plastic gods.

The long distance drivers of India have various strange theories about the laws of driving. Speed is of the essence. This often involves a diet of uppers and downers to give them maximum driving hours. It also means that the entreaties painted on sharp corners to 'Be gentle on my curves' and 'Hurry home but do not make your wife a widow' are ignored as the lorries scream around the corners, in cartoon fashion, on two wheels. The cartoon frame comes to an abrupt end when the edge of the road gives way and the psychedelic *Kama Sutra* girls on the lorry doors end up staring at the sky from the bottom of a crevasse. The steep slopes along the road are pock-marked with the carcasses of Tata-made lorries. These lorries also belch an illegal amount of diesel that hangs in the mountain air and coats the roadsides in an ugly layer of dark silt. You cannot wander along the roads of The Kulu Valley without being in continuous danger of bursts of pollution, or of death.

The towns of Manali and Kulu, and their satellite villages, have a constant population of tourists who while bringing much needed money to the area, also bring their own breed of pollution. It is not an act carried out by any particular backpacker or trekker, but the roll on effect that tourism has on an agricultural community that has no control over building development. Traveller's cheques were like a drug to the local people. The apple growers built hotels in their orchards, and watched the money roll in as the apple trees came down. They did not worry too much about what the buildings looked like or whether their sewage or plumbing was being put down properly.

The Kulu Valley has clung on to its beauty but it is the jaded beauty of a middle-aged woman, who has not been able to protect her asset with careful living. The Parvati Valley, that forks away from the Kulu, is still preserved and is a reminder of what the Kulu was like before it became a main stop on the hippie trail.

Parvati was the beautiful wife of the Hindu god Shiva, The Destroyer and Reproducer, whose cosmic dance shook the universe and created the world. In a lull between his various manifestations Shiva fathered two sons. There was a bad moment when Shiva returned from a celestial sojourn to find his exquisite Parvati taking a bath in the presence of a young man. In a bewildered rage, Shiva struck off the head of the young man, without stopping to think that his son, Ganesh, might have changed from a boy into a man during the long period that he had been away. Parvati forced Shiva to bring her son back to life. Being a potent god this did not present a problem, but the only way he could do it was to give the young man the head of the first living thing that passed by. It was, of course, an elephant. So Ganesh got his elephant's head and Parvati got her valley to calm her nerves with its sparkling river, clean air, sulphur springs, and with wild mint, thyme and garlic on the hillsides. She also got the more discerning hippies who settled there, and have now been there for so long that it is almost impossible to tell the difference between the locals and the new age settlers.

One of the reasons that the hippies decided to stop in Parvati is that there are fields of Marijuana; not just the odd patch, but acres of fields. The sadhus (ascetic holy men) in the temples at the sulphur springs have the same spaced expression on their faces as the pretty Italian hippie who sat outside the rest house, diligently applying thick black kohl around her eyes with the intensity of an open heart surgeon. They are all on a great trip, though the holy men seem to smile most of the time while the hippies just look rather bemused.

The rest-house at Kasol, in the neck of the Parvati Valley, was our last contact with Paddy, and with lavatories, until we got to the other end. Supper on the veranda of that rest-house seemed very safe. Paddy's truck was sitting there, red and shiny, and representing a reliable way of getting from A to B. The porters were camped down in one of the outhouses in a soft buzz of conversation and gambling. Karma and Sonam bustled back and forth producing food out of a tiny black hut. The sky was clear and fish belly pink. One solitary sunflower hung its head. Paddy was talking at high speed but the rest of us were rather quiet. Above the *dhal* and vegetable curry was the smell of trepidation. We were about to set out without Paddy and we were not quite sure where we were going.

We went to bed with our climbing boots neatly parked at the end of our sleeping bags. Will was met by a large, waving spider when he unzipped his bag. He remained calm while Paddy leapt around the room in a fit of terror, dancing on the camp beds like a banshee with a bad omen.

On 5 September 1992 we set off on foot. The Spiti Valley had officially just been opened for those who held the right visa. It had taken a year of wrangling to get that visa. A year of frustrating conversations with officials who nodded their heads in the way that plastic dogs do on the back shelves of cars. They nodded until their heads nearly fell off but they did not mean 'yes'. They meant 'maybe', or 'we will have to see' or, 'I am not sure that you are talking to the right person'. It had been a year of stops and starts, temper-tantrums and over-excitement; of postponement and holding my breath and counting to ten at the Indian Tourist Office. Selfishness had made me hope that each hitch meant that fewer others would be getting permits at the same time as I was. I had been assured that we would be the first outsiders into the Spiti Valley since time immemorial, but I had raised my eyebrows, and ruminated on flying pigs.

It was warm and the Parvati Valley had a film set quality. The woods smelt of moss and damp leaves and the fields had a fuzz of alpine flowers floating over the stubby grass. We were on a clean path that pulled us up out of the valley bottom. It was an easy, swinging walk.

Karma stopped at a chai hut in the early afternoon. We lined the path behind him, propped against rocks, in various states of undress. The morning cloud had broken into muggy sunshine and our t-shirts hung in the channels of our backs. Will could strip down further than the girls; his neat spare tyre getting its final airing before being whittled down by the climbing and *dhal* diet. A small girl stood by the opening of the chai hut and lifted her worn dress over her head as the owner produced glasses of chai for the tourists. Nobody minded, least of all her; she was using the thin material to protect her head from the sun and it was the most logical course of action. There was no coyness or calculation. She had a piece of material and it was of more use on her head than on her body, so she put it there. We left them with a pile of empty chai glasses. I looked over my shoulder several times as we walked away and the girl remained motionless, with her dress still over her head.

I am ignorant about drugs. I have been all over the place: up and down the dark alleys of Bangkok, around the syringe dumps of Sydney and the narcotic stops of India, but I do not think that I have ever been offered more than a hood-eyed toke. This ignorance seems to have been my protection. When asked if I smoke I drift into a soliloquy about cancer being the scourge of our family; this is enough to send any good pusher scurrying away.

We had been walking through tall green fields for several hours on that first afternoon. Our line had become straggled and I was walking ahead with Karma. I did not put great faith in his knowledge of flora and fauna in English. I had once asked him the name of a brilliant yellow flower that I had been about to crush underfoot. It had looked like a small orchid to me. He had looked at me sagely and told me that it was a 'Meentan Flo'. I bored Will with my exclamations on the Meentan Flo when one next came into sight. We met up with Paddy at the end of the trek and I alighted on one of these yellow flowers while walking with him. Like a pouter pigeon I puffed up with my knowledge. When he managed to stop laughing he told me that the yellow beauties were indeed orchids and Karma's accent had made mountain flower sound like Meentan Flo. I was not going to risk the same thing again. I just admired the spread, spiky leaves that we were walking through and wondered why the locals let these weeds grow in such orderly profusion. For weed it was; acres of cannabis. I was given a diatribe about being a cannabis virgin in the face of this exquisite crop of mellowness.

Chastised and clutching cannabis leaves to press into my diary and to keep as a form of reference, I walked into Pulga, another bastion of hippiedom. Why indeed should they go any further when surrounded with so many acres of grade A smokes to contemplate, while discussing the demise of the globe?

The people of Pulga are farming families in the same business as the opium farmers of Chiang Rai in Thailand. Their kind of crop matures into something with a more explosive moral message than wheat cereal on the breakfast table. They are dictated to by the drug Mafia who give them a quota to fill. If they do not achieve this target they are penalised; the Overlords pay them less per kilo. For the farmer this means that he does not have enough money to feed his family or for effective replanting for the following harvest. A downward spiral starts. This makes the men of Pulga diligent farmers. They do not see photographs of junkies, nor do they understand the stranglehold of the drug barons on the youth markets of the world.

Rather than being a nuisance in Pulga the hippies act as a useful quality control. The farmers can judge the grade of their crop by the standard of conversation stemming from the cannabis smokers. The less sense they make the better the crop and the more money the farmer will make to feed his children. ·

The children of Pulga are savvy Mowgli characters who hunt in packs. They stared into our cameras like Tinseltown pros. They smiled, pouted, stuck their tongues out and looked straight into Will's lens. They had no reservations about taking the camera from around his neck and shooting the telephoto lens in and out at each other in a phallic fashion accompanied by lewd, excited laughter. The more attention that we gave them, the more aggressive and demanding they became. I watched them as they pulled at our clothes and tried to take things from our pockets. There seemed to be a lack of the innocence of childhood. This was a pompous conclusion. The innocence that I was mourning seems to be a luxury item that comes with the cotton wool effect of constant parental attention and a childhood of strict rules. These children of Pulga, India and other developing countries seem to pop out, learn to walk and then fend for themselves in acquisitive packs. They would cause revolutions in the nursery schools of the West. They dress, feed and wash themselves. By the age of three they have undammed streams of snot between their noses and their upper lips and degrees in street wisdom. They have been oohed and ahhed at by enough travellers to know how far they should allow their targets to get down a joint before they stick a begging hand in their face.

The children of the hippie trail villages have a select vocabulary for maximum gain. They break you in gently with a smiling 'Tata' or 'Hello'. You become a victim once you have returned their wave. Then the hunt is on and they are around you in a herd with a burning desire for 'pen pen' and 'sweet, choclite, sweet'. It seemed endearing that they wanted sweets and pens, instead of hard cash, until the World Health Authority informed us that we were rotting the young teeth of the Himalayas by handing out sweets. The cry of 'pen' appeared to be a cry for self-education. Not so; it was the cry of the entrepreneur set on getting a free supply for a pen stall and his or her junior entry into commerce (it tends to be much more of the 'his' than the 'her').

We stood in the middle of the village, conspicuous in our bright colours and cleanliness, gazing at the man on his hand loom and the cobalt blue of the village temple, while trying to avoid the grappling hands of the snotty children. The resident hippies stared at us with doleful expressions, despising us for our clean clothes, our enthusiastic exclamations and our lack of mellow attitude. They sat in the village centre in their grubby clothes and drew deep on their bong pipes with screwed up eyes and deep concentration. They hacked up their lungs and drew again as if they were going for the ultimate hallucination when their insides would actually drop out of their mouths into their laps in front of them. They viewed us with distaste as if we were the personifications of almost every reason that they had left society; we were dressed in mountain wear that would have caused huge amounts of pollution in its creation; we were swimming in a sea of porters paid for with corporate blood money, and we looked clean; in short, we were tourists and we were treading on their karma. We left the village to return to the rest-house with a Pied Piper string of children behind us. We were ripe for plucking whereas the hippies were old news.

Ella and Amanda hung back a little, seduced by the outstretched hands of the children. Two young boys were particularly persistent and crowded Ella when she squatted down amongst them. She took off the earrings that she was wearing and handed them to the boys. Her Indian love affair had really begun as she recorded passionately at the time:

We communicated with them in made-up sign language, gesticulations, facial expressions and lots of noise. They responded with glee. Especially two young boys, to whom I gave my earrings. They went whooping off down the path, leaping across the stream and pointing at the earrings in mid-flight (I gave them one each). They held them high like trophies and when they reached a woman and the rest of the children, there was an explosion of chattering and laughter. Their happy faces beamed back at us across the valley.

She was awed by the power of simple physical communication and the excitement caused by a pair of earrings that she had picked up on a wet Saturday afternoon for a song. When they got back to the rest-house Ella was animated and excited by the giving. Amanda was a little more guarded and allowed Ella to pour forth with the story of the earrings and the two boys.

As it was the last night in a rest-house we took advantage of the privacy that was on offer. Twenty pairs of eyes have a habit of getting everywhere when a girl is trying to do a strip wash without stripping. Indian women have the ability to wash themselves all over without exposing an inch of unsuitable flesh. Even in the poorest areas of Calcutta, where you might assume that modesty evaporated as the human condition plummeted, the women in the shanty towns manage to wash in the streets using a tin of water and a deft sari technique. We were not so dextrous and Will captured a line of naked girls, with rabbit expressions in his flash, trying to wash ineptly out of bowls of water.

We ate on the veranda looking out over the cannabis. When the candles had burnt down we went to bed behind useless mosquito screens peppered with holes that ground on their hinges every time a breeze came through. I put in my ear plugs to cut out the gambling banter of the porters and the moaning hinges, so I did not hear the thunder, or the heavy rain when it started.

It was blanket rain that wrapped us in damp. It was a bad sign. From the moment the porters woke up they were bickering about their loads. Everything had been soaked during the night's deluge. It was all now heavier; in the same way as a towel doubles its weight when it is wet. We ferreted to the bottom of our bags to pull out our wet weather gear. Amanda was totally equipped. Her nursery school experience made it second nature to bring a spare set for when Johnny wet his pants or, in the case of the Himalayas, when the clouds shed their load. Ella became a bag lady making a black dustbin liner her raincoat. The rest of us had various inadequate jackets that got wet and clung. Amanda and I had the advantage of the famous black Indian umbrellas 'for uses in rain and shine' purchased on the sly in Manali. We ate breakfast on the veranda looking out on the liquid view.

One of the porters came to me as I was brushing my teeth. He eyed the patch of toothpaste froth on my chin suspiciously then he waved his hands about, clasped his chest and made gasping noises, while pointing towards the gaggle of bickering porters. Once I had gleaned that he was not dying from agoraphobia it became clear that in the middle of the arguing was an ill man. I was being called on as 'the great white doctor'. My knowledge of medicine went as far as giving a rubber doll called Resussy Anne a breathy kiss during a first aid course at school, but in the eyes of the porters I was the boss memsahib so I must know how to cure a dying man.

The victim was crouched in the mud, clasping his whole body to his shins, and swaying backwards and forwards on his haunches. Each time he groaned a rattling sound came from his chest; the sound of marbles being shaken together in a bowl of jelly. There was silence amongst the porters when I approached. It was the silence of anticipation that you get at American healing conventions, before Elsa from Ohio throws aside her crutches, and rushes to the stage in ecstasy. I called for props and the medicine box appeared from Karma's cooking den. I remember rolling up my sleeves in the rain in the hope that it might give me some medical edge. I had little idea of what to do, but I did it with great confidence. I looked down his throat and tried to disguise my shock at the two rows of blackened stumps that were his teeth. The phlegm that coated his throat and tonsils looked dark and ominous. I tapped his back and chest and examined the deltas of blood vessels in the whites of his eyes. I felt his nose in case the same rule applied to humans as to dogs. His nose was hot.

I diagnosed bronchitis. It seemed the most obvious choice out of a host of diseases. I rubbed some Vicks on his chest and gave him a Paracetamol, with two more to take during the course of the day. I might as well have given him three Smarties, at least they would have tasted better. He got up on his stick legs and one of the other porters helped him to pull his load onto his back. He looked as if every particle of energy had been sucked out of him. I turned away, aware that there was nothing more I could do.

As we left the village the rain was beginning to turn the path into a bog. Even before we had passed the boundary fence I slid off the path into a deep trench full of chicken slurry. The hippies would have cheered if they had seen the filthy state in which I left Pulga.

We began to climb. The rain got heavier and the mud thicker. Each of us climbed in different ways. Ella and Amanda were deep into the revelations of mountain nature. Each new plant or flower that they found was an inspiration to go on up to find something more beautiful and rare. Each bloom was a thrill, the mud made them laugh, and they were amused by their panting as the climb became steeper. Jane set her jaw and weighed up the steep slope as a rival. I had done that before; fought against losing my breath and feeling my muscles giving up when the oxygen could not get to them fast enough. She looked determined but unhappy as she struggled up through the mud. Will lolloped along; his and Amanda's long legs giving them the advantage of stride over the rest of us.

It was a long climb up through mountain forest. We could see the end of the tree line where the dank smell of leaf mould and mud would disappear with the trees. It became a goal that we were heading for, where we would escape from the mud and into the hills. It would mean the re-emergence of our feet from the forest quagmire.

Mud must be the same the world over; it has the same ingredients of dirt and water. Yet Himalayan forest mud clings to you in a black layer, creeping into your pores, turning your skin an ugly grey. As you sink into it you are held vice-like. One of the quickest ways I have come across to wrench muscles from their moorings is to try to climb up while being wrestled back by this mud. It is just not the same as the kind of mud that I remembered almost skipping through on Scottish hills.

By late afternoon the rain had washed itself out. The fog sank down and the amber sun sat on the tops of the trees. The damp line of climbers began to steam; a group of sweaty work horses in a haze of condensation against the sun.

We walked into Khirganga. A toothy-faced character waved us into his wooden shack to take chai before we went up the clearing to 'make ablutions and become clean in the bubbling glories of the springs' as he expressed it. We were on the last gasp of the hippie trail where the sales patter is learned for the benefit of the long-haired lovers.

Khirganga has sulphur springs where you can lie back in the hot water, dream of Woodstock and emerge smelling of bad eggs. None of the hippie crowd were there when we arrived. It was the tail end of the season. The weather had become too fickle for the wise hippies to venture beyond Pulga.

I climbed up to the springs to avoid the blister examination taking place in the chai hut. The smell of sulphur got thicker. Steam hung over the baths. They were empty except for a sadhu. His long matted hair was piled on the top of his head in a girlish fashion. He was pushing himself from one side of the baths to the other, enjoying the rush of the warm water against his naked body. He smiled at me with an invitation in his eyes even though I had trespassed into the male section of the baths. 'Come in and try the water' his dilated pupils sparkled at me. He was hypnotic in this setting; the piled hair, the steam, the wide eyes and the idea of hot water on dirty skin. I forgot about the smell of bad eggs. I was trying to draw a picture of him in my head. I had my camera but I had no intention of strangling the moment.

Sadhus do not usually like to be photographed. These wandering holy men in pursuit of salvation believe that a camera takes away some of their spirit when the shutter closes. I murmured 'Babaji', a term of reverence used for holy men, and bowed my head. He stretched his thin arm out of the water towards me and spoke in a singsong patois, his eyes unfocused and glossy with tears. I did not want to break his movement. I stretched out my hand to him. He grabbed me in his bony fist and dragged me to the edge of the bath with surprising strength. I panicked and braced my legs against him. He let go as quickly as he had taken me and I went down hard on my bottom. He laughed and splashed me with the warm water. I blushed. I had mistaken his horseplay for a moment of spiritualism. He had just been making a mild point that girls should stick to the girls' side of the baths.

His laughter followed me as I slid down the hill through the mud. Will was coming up from the camp laden with cameras. I landed in a pile at his feet.

'Aren't they great?' He crouched down to look at the steam hovering over the baths through his lens.

'What? The baths, oh yes.'

'Is there anyone up there?' He asked. 'It would be great to get some of them in rather than us pasty-looking lot.'

'No there isn't. I mean there is no one but a sadhu.' I was still at his feet.

He looked at me in the way the sane look at the mildly deranged, shrugged and set off up the hill.

'What did he do, goose you or convert you?' He laughed without expecting an answer.

The sadhu was still there when we went back later to wash. It was beginning to get dark and he was still gliding about as he had been all afternoon. The baths were busy now. The porters had finished setting up camp and had climbed up the hill to wash. They were grouped around the men's side, peeling off their layers down to their loincloths and woolly shorts, the shapeless ones that appear on bony men in saucy 1930's seaside postcards. Some of the men were gaunt and emaciated, with hollow chests, jutting hips and pin legs; others had strong, healthy looking bodies.

We could no longer smell the sulphur. Like strong garlic, when we were all breathing it in we no longer noticed it. Once we had washed our hair, bodies and clothes, the sulphur was forgotten. We were elated by the bubbling water, and emerged from the baths goose-pimpled, in incongruous swimming suits, with piles of washed clothes steaming in the cold air. I walked past the sadhu. He was out of the baths and dabbing at himself nonchalantly with a corner of his damp loincloth.

'*Ap kaisé hain Babaji*? ("How are you holy one?")' I asked him trying to make amends for my earlier misjudgement.

He looked up and stared at me, his soulful eyes crinkling into a smile. He said nothing and once again I blushed and shuffled away. He called out to my retreating figure, when I was almost out of earshot. '*Bahut, bahut* – (. . . "Very, very . . .")' I turned to hear the end of the sentence but there was no more. He smiled and shrugged, upright and warm in the evening cold as I shivered in a hastily donned fleece jacket: something beyond Gortex was keeping him warm.

This man was one of a curious breed. Any traveller to the Indian subcontinent will have come across sadhus or swamis. They come in different varieties, according to their sectarian allegiances. Some have shaven heads and a simple ochre loincloth or robe. Others allow their hair to lie matted on their shoulders, or wear it coiled into a lank top knot like my friend at the sulphur baths. They daub themselves in paint; yellow or white stripes that dry and crack across their foreheads like children's poster paints. In the boiling sun you will find one of them sitting under a tree; a rubber band man in the lotus position, under several layers of clothing and complicated wooden bead necklaces. On a cold mountain pass a sadhu will skip towards you with just a loincloth hanging from his hip bones.

The word '*sadhu*' means saint, but the class of sadhus and swamis is made up of ordinary men (and a few women) of many faiths. They leave their homes, families and material life to follow the severe deprivations of ascetics in search of enlightenment. Some pursue the disciplines of yoga, hence they are called yogis; others are disciples of the Hindu gods Shiva and Vishnu; and the Bikkhus are the Buddhist believers.

You may find them squatting on the *ghats* (landing steps on the river) of Varanasi or under a bush in the desert; usually surrounded by their few worldly possessions; a staff (*danda*), a squat-bellied waterpot (*kamandalu*), an alms bowl and a rosary, and perhaps an extra threadbare loincloth and a fire tong. The tong is believed by some to have an old parable attached to it that came from the rigorous ascetic Jain sect. It is a parable that teaches that we must not inflict pain on one another or any living thing.

The tale starts with a man who lifts a bowl of burning coals with a pair of tongs. He carries the bowl to a group of 363 founders of philosophical schools. Each one of these philosophers has differing sets of beliefs and theories. The man with the coals gathers the group around him and he asks each philosopher to take the bowl from him (parable lore does not tell us how the coals stayed burning for the duration). One by one the philosophers pull back from the bowl crying out that they will burn their hands.

'Ah,' says the man, 'We have found one true principle that can be applied to everyone: all creatures are averse to pain. He who causes pain to any creature will himself suffer many pains.'

These spiritual wanderers are not only emaciated saintly figures, but there are also fortune tellers and magicians amongst them, who gather at the fairs and festivals around India, to look into the future of any tourist for a suitable price. Many of them have an uncanny ability to tell you gory details about your past life and loves. Once they have got you into a nervous state of anticipation, and they have extracted money from you, they give you a wishy washy future reading which could be translated any way you choose. There are real soothsayers among their number who are almost ethereal characters with eyes that shoot into your subconscious. These genuine articles should not be confused with the money-grabbing fakes.

If there is a sect with high ideals it does not take long for the criminal element to creep in and milk it for all its worth. Among the sadhus are those who have taken the guise of the nomadic lifestyle for various dubious ploys. Some rip off the tourists at fairs, others wallow in a constant cannabis stupor, or embark on frenetic sex marathons with free thinking, gap travellers determined to really widen their horizons.

As a result of some of the strange stories circulating about raunchy sadhus, the ascetics are often given unsympathetic press. Every sect has its false followers, but the rotten fruit should not make us view every sadhu with a cynical eye. I am not sure whether the sadhu at the baths was the real McCoy but he had an aura of calm that went beyond the balming effects of the bubbling sulphur water and the fields of marijuana.

The dramas in the camp that evening were twofold and I was the source of the first. The late light was flat and the slope down to the camp had become a dew-dressed slide. My legs shot up around my ears and I landed on my left knee with the crunch of someone pulling a chicken wing apart. It was a familiar sound. I had heard it six months earlier in Austria when my skis collided with a large rock. I had come down the mountain on a snow plough, and cried when the surgeon told me about the operation that I would need. The ligaments in my knee looked like knicker elastic. I was shown the gruesome spectacle of the operation on video, courtesy of keyhole surgery. The inside of my knee was like Martin Scorsese at his most gruelling. The surgeon had looked at me with the careful bedside authority that comes with a private medical bill and told me that I would not be climbing any mountains for a while. I had tried to keep the sobbing to a minimum and set about a physiotherapy course that would have frightened off a few loud-mouthed footballers. As I was living on the fifth floor of a building with no lift, two months of dragging myself up and down the stairs on my rump had kept me fit, and given me a pair of shoulders to match the machismo of my climbing boots.

To hear that same crunch again three days into the climb to Spiti made me feel immediately sick. I lay in the grass moaning pathetically. Amanda was near at hand and she heard my whimpering. She was calm and helped me to get up, pumped me full of arnica (a homœopathic healer) and left me in the green womb of my tent.

Karma arrived at the height of my self pity. Amid the sighing we had a lengthy discussion about sending me back with two porters to help me through the mud. He is a wise man. I think he realised that the idea of having to skid down through the thickening mud terrified me, and that it might inspire me to heal fast. He left me to another flood of tears once he was out of earshot. The boredom of crying sent me to sleep. I was still undecided about what would happen the following day, but I prayed to the valley gods for a bit of celestial intervention for my selfish cause.

I may have been undecided about how the next day would dawn but my subconscious did not swerve; nothing was going to stop me getting into Spiti and the mud on the path up might not be so thick as the mud on the way down.

My only other immediate problems that night were a full bladder, a bad knee, and twenty hawk-eyed porters. I had to abandon my shoes so that my toes could grip in the mud. I found a bald bush and managed to balance my throbbing leg on a rock. I tried to ignore the porters, though I think any titillation would have been limited by the curtain of rain that had descended on us once again.

The second drama unfolded in the porters' tent. A pale-skinned man had appeared in the camp. He had European features and his eyes seemed sometimes blue, other times green; but his language was a strange dialect that seemed to be a marriage between Tibetan and back slang. He was a man from Malana.

Malana is a village within its own valley. It looks up to the peak of Deo Tibba. From the top of the nearby Chandrakhani Pass you can just see the serrated peaks that fringe the Spiti Valley. Malana is a mosaic of strange history and apocryphal tales. The Divine myth tells the story of Jamlu, the main god of the Malana Valley. He was carrying a casket of gods to the end of the habitable world, more commonly known as the Kulu Valley. He paused for a moment on the top of the Chandrakhani Pass and a breeze blew open the lid of the casket, scattering the gods through the Kulu Valley. The human myth involves Alexander the Great. He and his troops passed near Malana on their descent of the Himalayas. The lushness of the valley after the arid tundra of their forced march seduced some of Alexander's men and they settled in the village. So a new stock of blue eyes and blond hair came among the dark skins of the Himalayas.

The passing of the centuries usually filters out distinctive foreign blood in intermarriage but not in Malana. The village closed in on itself. It created its own dialect and its own government and laws. The people of Malana are allowed to intermarry as many times as they like to keep their bloodline pure; the word bigamy does not seem to exist in their dialect. They protect themselves from the prying eyes and ears of strangers and tourists by hurling stones and abuse at anyone who starts to come too close to their village life. Many are the travellers' tales of victimised trekkers who have been on the receiving end of mud, stones or rotten vegetables. After a couple of *bhang lassis* (an iced yoghurt drink made with ganga) at Pete's café the stories get wilder and more violent, but the message is the same: the people of Malana do not want to let in the outside world. To have one of them in the camp, a couple of day's walk from Malana, without any of his fellow stone-throwing villagers, was a rarity.

Karma translated the conversation to me. It may have been tinted en route into English, due to the fact that nobody quite understood the Malana dialect; and Karma's amazement at the whole episode made his English poor and my Hindi even more ragged than usual. I got the impression that there had been a ribald volley of questioning from the porters, who were all keen to know the advantages of multi-marriage, and whether it led to a sex life of constant euphoria. The man from Malana had been recalcitrant about his replies, especially to the smuttier inquiries. Karma assured me that he had not looked like a man awash with the glow of sexual conquest.

Infuriated that I had not been there to witness the cross-examination of the stranger in our camp I asked Karma whether the stranger had spent the night with the porters. Karma shrugged and said that he had been too busy to notice. He had made fresh mountain bread for breakfast.

I had offended Karma on two counts; first of all it was beneath the guides to share a tent with the porters, who they regarded generally as a bunch of animals with voracious appetites and rotting lungs. This meant that there was no reason why he should know the movements of the man from Malana. Secondly, the bread for breakfast was a vain attempt to rouse what Karma and the guides regarded as my pathetic appetite. It was too complicated to go into the gloomy details of an old Indian encounter with out of date antibiotics that had given me an unattractive allergy to flour and yeast. It meant that I never touched the fresh chapattis, papadums, *rotis* and hot doughnutesque *puris*, even though they all made me drool. As a result they all thought that I survived on raw onion salad and fresh air. It had taken me two years to convince Karma of his brilliance as an innovative high altitude cook, but that I could just not eat his food without risking the violent wrath of my gut.

Karma softened a bit when he saw my sad expression and the melodramatic bandage on my knee. He suggested that the stranger might well have stayed because of the rain. There had also been a great deal of gambling and drinking going on in the porters' tent and around the fire until late into the night. Karma shrugged again and volunteered that the stranger's stay might well have encouraged the excesses among the porters.

Jane stared with bleary accusation from her sleeping bag, disgusted by my early morning chatter with Karma. She looked at the bed tea that Karma had brought with distaste and returned to her chrysalis state beneath the hood of her bag.

As I was crippled by the size of the bandage around my leg, quite apart from any injury, there was little chance that I was going to make a silent survey of the porters' tent to see if the man from Malana was there. I stomped down to their big tent. There was a concert of hacking and throat-clearing and a smell akin to both a stable and a football changing room. One of the younger porters stuck his head out of the tent flap and smiled at me. It was Shribadur. He normally wore a large fur hat, but it was now just his rumpled hair and smiling face that greeted me.

'The man from Malana?' I waved my hand towards the rancid interior of the tent, hoping that they were going to produce a blond Caucasian out of the gloom.

Shribadur put his hands on his belly and laughed with so much air that I thought he would choke.

'You want be wife Malana?' He managed to gasp through his laughter.

'No, no, I just thought it might be interesting to meet him.' I knew that I had lost him. 'Has man gone?' I asked.

'Take . . .' He pointed at the palm of his hand to indicate money and then made a fan of his fingers to display cards. So the man from Malana had whipped our boys at cards and then run off with his hoard.

'Malana man very good . . .' Shribadur ran his hands up and down the air, fondling the space between our bodies. 'Many wives practice.' He cackled again. I waved my hand in disapproval, but laughed. How I would have enjoyed meeting the Casanova card sharp from Malana. How wise he was to have fled the prying tourists with their questions and probing cameras.

[4]

THE STEEP SILENCE

O UR strange family was extended at Khirganga. We had made the mistake of feeding too much *jalebi* (deep-fried syrup pancakes) to a good looking mongrel as we wandered the streets of Manikaran at the start of our journey. I had pounced on the jalebi man and his frying pan, determined to gorge on his sickly wares, before the deprivations of mountain life. Having bought a large bag even I, the jalebi queen, had been unable to get half way through the mound. So we had a fan seduced by jalebis. This young bitch was joined in Khirganga by a handsome golden retriever with a stub tail that tried to loop like a husky dog's. He had fought off the rabble that had descended on our young innocent in a sexual flurry of tails and bared teeth when we reached the sulphur springs. The golden retriever had been her champion and they lay outside the tent while we were having breakfast as if they had been with us all their lives. There was a surge of pubescent canine passion brewing.

As is the English wont, these animals had to be named immediately so that we could love them as dear fluffy packages with labels. The dog became Black, in a flood of creative thinking, and the bitch K Nau, *'nau'* being the Hindi for 'nine'.

Ella had been my crutch that morning. One of the strings to her bow was dabbling in holistic healing and massage. We sat outside my tent in the rain while the porters began to assemble the bedraggled camp onto their backs. She ran her hands over my knee, hovering just above the skin, murmuring deep things to drag all the tension and spasm out of the injury. At the end of the session she patted it like a naughty child. It responded, and once trussed up like a turkey, performed all day as an old warrior.

It was Jane's birthday. She had greeted the morn with a short, sharp expletive. She is not a morning girl. In chalet skiing party fashion we tried to be jovial at breakfast. Karma produced a fine round of fresh bread off the fire, and a present from Paddy that turned out to be a pretty Kulu shawl, bright with naive embroidery. I gave her a Himachal hat; a flat round hat with an old band of embroidery across the front favoured by the men of the valley and an essential part of every tourist's return luggage. I planted it on her head at a jaunty angle. I got the expression that usually withers you when you try to put a Christmas-cracker paper hat on a blue-rinsed maiden aunt.

We left Khirganga in the rain. There was a pathetic attempt to frighten away the dogs, but they were determined, and we could no more resist their damp, limpid expressions than we could have dispensed with the services of our army of porters.

The continuing deluge had turned the mud into setting cement. I gave up my stalking position at the front of the party and crept along behind, talking to my knee with firm encouragement. It was calmer at the back. While pace-setting through the thick mud in the forest I always felt that Will was just behind my shoulder striding to overtake me. He now loped in the front at his own comfortable pace while the rest of us straggled behind him. The treeline was just above us, and the rain stopped.

We broke out of the forest into the high meadows.

Old relations have a tendency to have water-stained paintings of what the landscapes of Europe looked like in the midst of the last century, usually courtesy of Great Uncle Edward and his paint box. Many of these scenes seem to be the Swiss Alps, complete with tiny figures in Alpine frocks, residing over flocks of goats or cows. These pictures have common themes such as bubbling streams of crystalline water, skies unhazed by pollution, and verdance that could only have been the result of a constant chlorophyll orgy. This was the scene that we walked into and Walt Disney would have been proud. The dogs frolicked through wild thyme, garlic, and floral paraphernalia in startling primary colours. We set off through a field of yellow flowers, that came up above our shoulders, with steam coming off our clothes; the sun had broken through.

We came down to a river. It had looked small and picturesque from the top of the valley, but when we reached it the water had grown from the sweet silver trickle that we had first seen before we climbed down to it. There was no crossing point. There were two large rocks that stood proud of the water; the distance between them probably the same as jumping three average pavement squares. Pavement squares are easy to jump if you are on a pavement, but if you are hopping from one wet rock to another the distances seem multiplied by the danger. After the rocks there was a larger gap, so there was a sodden log across the water.

I was at the back and rounded the corner to our crossing place to find Ella dangling from Will's hand. Her bare legs were being smashed between two rocks below her. Her hair was dark against her white skin and the shock of bright blood. Will was shouting at her to grab his wrist because he was losing his grip on her hand. It was clear that Ella was not going to hear anything that was shouted at her. Her eyes were fixed with terror on the churning water that was throwing her body from one rock to another. Karma was hopping up and down on the furthest rock like a mad Scottish dancer. The rest of us stood and watched in silence as Karma joined Will. They braced themselves against the edge of the rock, relying on Ella's diminutive weight, and the suction of the water to act as a fulcrum.

She came out of the water easily and was carried like a doll to the grass on the other side. The rest of us crossed carefully and huddled around her. She was frozen. The river ran straight off a glacier. She had been hanging in it long enough to drop her body temperature and turn her the foam white of the river. Her wounds and bruises were patted and tended, and her wet clothes laid around her to dry in the sun. There were some wild strawberries growing among the grass, some of them crushed in our frenzied activity around Ella. I found some that had not been trampled and we ate them. Ella held them in her hand, staring at them as if they were the first strawberries that she had ever seen. She needed a cup of sweet tea, provided by a stalwart nanny figure, rather than those dots of mountain fruit.

She climbed back into her old clothes and forced one of those 'I'm all right' smiles. She is one of those girls who has worn 'I'm all right' smiles all her life, whether dealing with a genuine life crisis or an annoying driver in a traffic jam. Her little body, with the wet clothes clinging to it, set off up the hill again. There was not much else that anyone could do except follow her.

'Lucky she is a Buddhist,' said Jane.

'Why?' asked Amanda.

'Because you wouldn't have caught me climbing back into those filthy wet clothes on my birthday if you paid me,' Jane replied.

'It's not her birthday,' frowned Amanda.

Jane rolled her eyes in annoyance. Amanda glared. For the first time there was a tangible sense of anger, flooding in the wake of the release from the panic after Jane's fall.

Will looked at the group of women in spate, and adopted an expression of bemusement, to protect himself from any involvement.

'Come on, girls, the W.I. session is over, let's go,' he chirped.

The ire was turned on him, but he was walking too fast to feel it boring into his back. The leaden atmosphere was pricked by a field of head high flowers, fluffy yellow chicks on long stalks that rose above as we walked through them, so that we looked up at the sky through a canopy of canary blooms. As Ella was the accident victim she was dictating the mood of the afternoon. She was delighted by the flower field. The sun shone, the dogs frolicked and, for a while, the ragged peaks did not look so ferocious.

The sides of the valley were beginning to peer at us, soaring on either side, giving the same impression that I used to get from very tall, elderly relations when I was a child. When we came into the next camp-site there was an outcrop of rock high above us at the climax of a jagged ridge. On the edge of the outcrop were some Buddhist prayer flags, faded and snagged by the weather. Karma was in front of me, trotting along with the same comfortable gait as the dogs.

'Who takes the prayer flags all the way up there?' I asked him.

'Sometime the village, sometime the monk.' He shrugged.

'How do they get up there?' I strained my head back to see if there was a visible path to the outcrop. There was nothing but the raw rock.

'Sometime walk, sometime fly.' Karma shrugged again and then giggled. He turned around and crinkled his face at me. 'Sometime they are there and no one know how. Maybe Buddha carry them up.'

Maybe he did. It was either that or an extraordinary act of faith that took the prayer flag planters up high into the cruellest reaches of the mountains. Theirs is a powerful faith that steps beyond the mean route of religion.

Buddhism has crossed the world in ever increasing circles since the great Emperor Asoka of India (234–198 BC) spread it through his empire to Burma, Thailand, Sri Lanka, Korea, China, Vietnam, Nepal, Tibet, Central Asia and Japan.

My knowledge on the subject was sketchy. It seemed a good opportunity to take Ella's mind off her scratches and woes. I dog-trotted to catch up with her.

'Who was Buddha?' I asked.

'He was just a man.' It was too simple an explanation.

'Is that it?'

She stopped and looked at me to see if I appeared receptive. She drew her conclusion and walked on.

'There's no doubt that he lived, but he wasn't a god or a saviour, just a man dissatisfied with the pain and anxiety of life. 'Do you know, even when he was dying he was still at it? He had his favourite disciple, Ananda, with him. With his last gasps he asked why he should bother to keep his body if the Noble Truth would exist forever, even then he was selfless', she said.

'No, I didn't know that. How did he die?' I asked.

'I think he got food poisoning or overdid the rice. But he had a good run for his money; he was eighty when he died in 483 BC. Socrates was only six when Buddha died.' She gave me a look to say that I should mull over this fact.

'How old was he when he saw the light?' I asked.

'The actual date was when he was sitting under the Bodhi tree but he built up to it over a long period. He became disenchanted with his privileged background when he was a young man.

'I think he was born around 563 BC. He was a prince you know; Prince Siddhartha Gautama in the village of Lumbini, somewhere near the modern border of Nepal and India. His father was the rajah up there. The young prince grew up with all the advantages of coming from a wealthy background; a bit of a golden boy really.'

'Did he have a mother?' I asked.

'Of course he did. There is an enormous amount of mystery and myth about his birth. Some people think that he sat in the heavens before his life on earth and hand-picked his parents, based on their suitable past histories and credentials. Others say that his mother, Maya, died seven days after giving birth as, having produced a Buddha, there was nothing more that she could do.

'I think his father overdid the parenting bit. He was terribly overprotective about his son, sheltering him almost completely from the outside world. Even Buddha admitted that he was very spoilt during his early life. He had different palaces for different times of the year. When the Monsoon started he used to trot off to his wet weather palace with a bevy of dancing girls.' Ella laughed at the thought of the harem in the rain.

'Did he get married?' I wanted to get down to the nitty gritty.

'Yes, he married when he was still very young, and he managed to hang on to the dancing girls as well. His wife had a baby boy and his father called him Rahula. The name translates as "chain". It seems to be one of the early signs that he was falling out of love with his peacock lifestyle.

'He started to go on journeys away from his palaces, coming face to face with the real world of suffering, pain and death. He could not work any of it out and just kept coming up against a wall when he questioned the fate of man. On his fourth journey he met a monk, a simple man with a begging bowl, who seemed perfectly content in his wanderings. The prince realised that his glossy life was all a sham. He became determined to find something better and higher; the true knowledge.'

'What happened to his wife?' Once again the nosey question.

'He sloped off in the middle of the night, leaving his wife and baby, and he took up a tough life of self-denial, yoga, starvation and torment; all to try and unite himself with the origins of the world. He went off to Uruvelor in North India where he began to gather a troupe of followers around him. He spent six years bending himself in and out of yoga positions and almost starving himself to death, but it just didn't do the trick.

'His main aim was to rid man of the cycle of death and rebirth. He lost patience with all the deprivation. He extracted himself from his yoga bend and dived into a bowl of rice. His troupe were horrified that he was eating and wearing clothes again so the gaggle of starved bones upped and left him.

'This was his big break really. He remembered how he had meditated at home under his favourite apple tree. He realised that this was the way forward. He found a fig tree and sat underneath it. Well, that was the Bodhi tree and that was where he reached enlightenment.'

'Did he just float off to heaven then?' I asked.

'No, he went through the usual thing of being tempted by a demon. It wasn't forty days in his case, but the foul Mara tried to get him to enter Nirvana, the heaven of heavens, without passing his great message of enlightenment on to the common man. The god, Brahma, stepped in and persuaded Buddha that he must pass on his teaching. Buddha gave in and this is where his "wheel of teaching" was set in motion.' Ella had her hands pressed to her face in her enthusiasm for her subject.

'Do Buddhists believe in miracles; I mean could a Buddhist fly?' I had to find out how the prayer flags got up so high.

She followed my sight-line up to the flags and laughed.

'I don't know. Perhaps they can.' She walked on, still laughing.

We camped just below the prayer flags in a meadow surrounded by seven waterfalls. There was a general air of merriment; the dogs had almost conquered the sex act, Ella was still alive and, for once, the porters were not sodden. It was also still Jane's birthday.

A delegation was sent from the porters in search of healing hands. Ella and I rubbed Vicks vigorously into the chests of the iller men squatting around the fire. It was a painful exercise for them. Their skin was stretched in a thin, fatless covering over a frame of tired bones. It felt that if we rubbed too hard, it might just tear away from the jagged edges of their chests. They showed their gratitude by holding our wet clothes in front of their fire while we muttered and wondered about the curious wasting effect on the porters caused by bronchitis at high altitude.

Karma had bought Jane a birthday cake under Paddy's guidance. How they managed to find a rich Dundee fruit cake amongst the withered chickens in the Manali bazaar is a mundane miracle. Karma showed us the cake with great pride while he was bubbling up the afternoon brew of chai. In true chintzy memsahib fashion, I picked some of the meadow flowers, assisted by an embarrassed Karma, and covered the cake under a floral blanket peppered with bugs. Filled with a sense of artistic achievement I set off to find Jane so that we could sing 'Happy Birthday' to her.

She had disappeared into the distance behind a rock, with her book, to read and squat. The cake had to wait for two chapters of Agatha Christie. She finally returned, enervated by her straining labours and the Christie crime web. We sang and cut the cake and the sun went down.

The petals of our personalities were beginning to unfold. Now that we had been through the first part of the journey we seemed to feel more comfortable about stripping away the outer colours. The initial excitement of leaving had softened, to be replaced by a daily routine that we were comfortable enough with to allow our own traits to come through. Will had started to talk to himself, in an unabashed fashion, as he had on an earlier trek that we had been on together. When we had pitched camp he could be heard in animated conversation with himself, going into detailed discussions about his cameras. Ella and Amanda were established in their two-man tent as were Jane and I; the Buddhist tent and the gentile one, with Will as the atheist quarter. The smell of his sleeping bag in the morning, his constant monologue and his sex meant that poor Will had his tent pitched down wind from the female majority.

As the sole man in the gang of five, Will had been subjected to eagle observation to see if he shambled into a climbing romance. There had been red herring signals, on one of the first nights in Manali, when Amanda and he had gone into a huddle to discuss the glories of Buddhism. It seemed to have been a fleeting high altitude thing.

I had begun to worry about mountain romps and the complications of sexual politics, or indeed sex at all, in the thin mountain air. The ugly tales of emotional rupture that come back from jolly chalet skiing-holidays, had made me wonder how much these sexual intrigues would be increased by throwing a few thousand feet of altitude and basic living into the equation. All these concerns were unfounded. We were a far too selfish lot to entertain the idea of entertaining someone else while trying to stagger up mountains. Also the complications of our own love lives back home left little room for light-hearted travelling affairs.

We were safe celibates, though the intensity of Buddhist Tantrics, and their seemingly sexual meditations, did sometimes frill our interest. This was stemmed by our lack of patience to go into a meditation anywhere close to being deep enough to achieve their mental orgasms: a tempting mixture of two powers, the male and female or the Being and the Becoming. The bustling female is the Being element (in Tantric Yoga, the base of the spine), and the foresighted male is the Becoming (seated in the mind). When the busy female element enlivens the spine the energy travels and unites with the male mind in an explosion of colour and understanding.

Tantric Buddhism sees the body as a vehicle of enlightenment and so it is sacred. It can alter the mind through movement of the limbs and intense breath control. In a man this can go as far as controlling the passage of his sperm. Thus, in Tibetan Tantric Buddhism a sacramental performance of sex can be a means to enlightenment. This belief teaches that sexual desire can be channelled away from the exhausting goal of base human orgasm, and the energy concentrated on sublime realisation. Under the careful guidance of a guru, a Tantric student can be taught to control his ejaculation. This sexual power is re-directed inwardly so energising and invigorating the *chakras* (the nerve centres of the body).

One rite of this Tantric teaching suggests that a man and a woman sit opposite each other in the lotus position. They allow their bodies to be aroused by the sensations of covering each other with flowers, lighting incense to each other, and offering wine. As the wine lulls, and the breath transcends strictures of self-consciousness, the woman moves to sit on the man's lap with her hands clasped around his neck, while the man supports her back with his palms as he enters her. They gaze into each other's eyes and do not move. The breathing, the physical and sexual contact intensify all the sensations to a height where no words are needed and not a sound is uttered, except for the rhythm of the breathing. Sexual desire and satisfaction have been replaced by an understanding of 'what is'.

In this bright, glorious celebration of sex the man and woman symbolise the noblest aspects of religious understanding. The man is *karuna*, active

[53]

compassion, and the woman, *prajna*, perfect wisdom. These intertwined figures are found in carved images all over areas of Tibetan Buddhism. They are looked on with great reverence as the unity of Nirvana and the world. It puts sex into a different arena; a level that delighted the flower children who converted to Buddhism in the 1970s.

We had escaped the dark cloud of sexual politics but this was by no means the only bogeyman on the horizon. There are several factors that combine when you throw people together in a vast landscape a long way from home, put them under freezing, damp tents night after night and feed them on horror stories of altitude sickness. You may not become undying friends, but a respect grows for one another in tandem with a healthy amount of competition. If any one of us had been placed on our own on one of those mountain sides, we would have given up. As a group of five the strong made the weak feel more resilient, and the calm soothed those of us who had a tendency to panic. The catalytic factor was a bullish determination to get through into Spiti.

We had all trotted around various London parks, proudly telling our friends that we were off to conquer high reaches, as we jogged gingerly around the Serpentine. We had sweated in gyms, bought ugly boots and expensive fleeces. We had looked through the books and had the jabs. What we had not done was forecast the worst deluge to hit southern Asia this century. As we set off into the mountains, Pakistan was declared a national disaster area as the rain churned over the Khyber Pass, tossing lives and homes out of its path.

Will was our news link. On that rare warm afternoon, he had been perched outside his tent drying his long johns on his body in the last of the sun. He had his radio clasped against his ear so that the aerial seemed to grow out of the back of his head. The miniature sound of the BBC World Service news theme was just audible. Will had an expression of profound concentration as he communed with the nice voice from Bush House.

'You know they are dying in their thousands over there?' He waved in the general direction of Pakistan.

'I know. Do you think it is going to come this way?'

The question remained unanswered until the end of the bulletin.

'They didn't give its route.' The radio was clicked off and the aerial pushed down but he remained in his Puck position on the rock, his knees clutched to his chest, as his long johns got cold and clammy in the sunset.

'Perhaps we've had it already?'

Will raised his eyebrows at my question.

'I doubt it, that was probably just a preview.'

'All the time that it has been raining down here it's been snowing up in the passes.' I was thinking about our lack of snow footwear.

'. . . great snaps.' Will's mind had wandered to Pakistan.

'We'll be all right, won't we?'

Will shrugged and sheathed himself into his tent.

It did not feel dangerous then. Stretched out around us was the meadow of Tunda Buj, with the background rhythm of the seven waterfalls, softened by distance to a gentle bubbling. The sunset had left the valley in grey while the peaks above us were washed in pink. Their brightness made them seem very close.

We were in remission.

Karma brought the tea the following morning, and, as my head appeared through the zip of the tent, he gestured expansively at the sky. It was blue.

The lack of rain gave us an injection of confidence. It did not last as the morning started with a sheer climb out of the valley, swinging from rock to rock. Will gave a short military lesson, straight out of a Sandhurst manual, about always keeping three points of contact with the rock that we were climbing. Ella was still raw from the river drama the day before. Climbing rock faces was not something that I had described to her during my idyllic sales patter in London.

Will walked past, told me not to look down, and set off upwards. I followed straight behind him, but it was impossible not to look down. Ella's voice followed me and I could hear the panic gathering in her throat. Looking down between my three points of contact I could see her flattened against a rock, the tips of her fingers white where they were trying to dig in. Karma was behind her, supporting one of her feet in his hand. She was kicking against his chest, trying to give herself some leverage and, in her fear, was unaware of how hard she was booting her protector. The porters were gathering below in an agitated group, keen to get up the rock face and on to the next obstacle.

We spent the majority of that day on our hands and knees, dangling off the rocks and crawling along a steep traverse, pinned to a narrow path by the sheer rise and fall of the loose scree above and below us. One of the group was crying, but there was nothing that the rest of us could do but continue to move forward. K Nau ran across the scree just above our path and a sheet of topsoil slid between us. The crying stopped and the only sound was the rattle of the scree running down the mountain. The dog ran on and the layer of scree rushed down behind her. By bending my head down I could see between my arms and legs. Karma was crouched behind me holding back Black. The skin on the dog's snout was pulled tight in a toothy grin as Karma hung on to a handful of neck to stop him joining in the scree flirtation. The crying resumed and we moved on.

We were upright by the afternoon; released into a meadow that appeared like a bowling green at the end of the arid scree. There were wild strawberries and stringy garlic plants. We were behind the porters and there was the smell of thyme where twenty pairs of feet walked over the meadow herbs.

That afternoon it was warm enough to lie in the grass with both sides of the tent open, to blow away the damp, stagnant air of the past few nights. Will was asleep in the sun, stretched out to his full length, long and pale against the small, dark porters hurrying up and down the slopes, in ant lines, collecting firewood. Some of them paused from the line and basked in the sun with their piles of firewood at their feet.

Jane was stretched over a warm rock with Agatha Christie, tapping her foot as the crime momentum mounted. Amanda had retreated to the valley side to go to war with her paints. She showed us an angry picture, later in the evening, that did not seem to be the same meadow that we were in, but a sad grey place from behind her mind.

Ella had also disappeared to stalk the valley, shouting at herself and trying to kick out her fears. I could see her slight form, wrestling its way up the steep side, sometimes stopping and crumpling for a few minutes. I lay in the grass and watched her punctuated progress. Then I realised what she was doing.

The sun was beginning to leave the valley and the evening shadow was following her. She was stopping in the sunlight, settling down to meditate, until the cold grey caught up with her, and goaded her further up the slope to the next warm patch; making her clamber higher each time to keep her place in the sun.

Between dusk and the following day there was a murder and a resurrection.

As Amanda and Ella returned from their mobile meditations, the rest of us sun slugs were beginning to retreat into our tents. Some shepherds came into the meadow with their goats and sheep. They were Gaddis, the nomadic denizens of the Himalayas, who drive their herds from the southern ranges up to the high pastures as the snows melt. They have the same slightly spiritual, slightly wild presence that seems to be shared by the wandering, high altitude clans of the world.

When you think you are alone on a high ridge, a Gaddi will appear from nowhere, dressed in homespun, often with a tired lamb peering from the fold of his tunic, its ears flopping as the shepherd walks. His small, tight physique will seem to glide over the terrain where you struggle, almost as if he were flying just above the ground.

The Gaddis usually leave their Gaddinis (womenfolk) in the homeland pastures, in the foothills around Chambra and Kangra where the Himalayas rise up from the Indian plains. Here the women and the children work the fields during the summer months while the men are away.

When you come across them they are usually friendly, and, if you are walking alone, they extend their mountain hospitality brewing up tea and chuckling at you, as you sit around their fire, stumbling through the barriers of communication.

The Gaddis, who arrived at Tunda Buj with the sunset, seemed pleased to have found fellow wanderers. They hobbled their rams and billies, and the ewes and she goats milled around their four-legged menfolk. The lead billy wore a large bell around his neck that jangled methodically as he cropped. When it got darker the bell ceased as the flock folded themselves down for the night. The Gaddis sank around the porters' fire and unbelted their *cholas* (tunics), so that they dropped from being knee-length to full height blanket robes for them to sleep in.

Karma was making fresh *puris* that puffed in the pan of hot oil like doughnuts. The camp-site had the sticky childhood smell of fairgrounds, and the shepherds and their flocks completed the comfortable, biblical scene.

The conversation flowed easily at supper. No one gave a lecture or a monologue. Various religions and creeds were given a colourful workout, opening a forum for Amanda and Ella on Buddhism. We had got to about number four of the Eightfold Buddhist path when the audience began drifting. We settled for the night and neither man nor beast stirred.

Sometime in the thick part of the night there was a clanging of bells and general ululations, but it was hard to tell whether it was part of a dream or outside in the darkness.

The morning light illuminated the scene of the crime. K Nau had been caught sheep molesting. It was impossible in the frenzy of dialects to ascertain what had happened. Karma and Sonam were on the receiving end of a spray of spittle from an aggressive trio of shepherds. The Gaddi tongue sounded like a series of bad tenor choir rehearsals and a gargling session. The porters were throwing their hands around in Nepalese and the guides seemed to be hopping between Tibetan, local Pahari dialects, Hindi, and English for expletives. Karma appeared to have become multilingual, and so, the giver of the most reasonable overview.

K Nau had been harrying the sheep. It was not clear whether she had killed one, and from the complete lack of forensic evidence, it seemed unlikely that she had even drawn blood. The shepherds' rage was based on the fact that some of their flock were said to be pregnant, and K Nau's antics would cause them to miscarry. It seemed strange for them to be pregnant just before the onset of winter. No common-sense argument could detract the shepherds; they were adamant about the Old Testament morals of an eye for an eye. So K Nau was to die in compensation for the potential future loss of foetuses. It was imperative that we did not intervene with the law of the Gaddis, so we left the rural court and packed our tents in silence.

Will was dry-eyed but morose and the rest of us were damp and tearful. Walt Disney would have smiled once more at our pre-emptive scene of mourning.

K Nau was strangled between two shepherds with a piece of rope. This took place over a low ridge just beyond the campsite. Will herded us away from it, but he could not cut out the asphyxiated screaming of the bitch. She leapt between the two men and some of her jumps rose above the ridge.

The porters were fascinated and hung around long after our melancholy little group had been led away by Chetram, our leading guide, and Karma. We were too affected by pet stress to think about the increasing difficulty of the climb that we were heading towards.

5

DYING MEN AND DOGS

A s we climbed higher Ella and Amanda's Buddhism seemed to be intensifying. Mountain altitude does appear to give everything a clarity that we miss at street level. The simple Buddhist sentiments seemed to sweep down from every prayer flag and pile of carved mantra stones. The complexities of the faith were slowly being ironed out as we questioned our two recent converts, while dog-earing their 'Buddhism for Beginners' books.

After Prince Siddhartha had been enlightened, and become the Buddha, he spent several more nights under the Bodhi tree, getting to grips with the machinations of the universe.

On the second night under the tree, Buddha understood the law governing the endless cycle of birth, death and rebirth.

On the third night he discovered the four noble truths that were to become the core of the Buddhist philosophy. When these are translated for the layman they fall into a simple quartet.

The first is the knowledge of suffering, and the miserable realisation that all existence is about suffering and pain.

The second reveals the origin of suffering to be ignorance and desire, hand in hand with longing and greed.

The third noble truth details the destruction of suffering, which is the central aim of Buddhism. This means a release from suffering and all the material things and emotions that cause it. This release is said to free us from the endless cycle of rebirth, or *samsara* as the Buddhists call it. When you are out of this loop there is the chance to enter Nirvana. This is the final rejection of our selfish nature and the complete absorption into the supreme spirit, or to put it simply, Buddhist heaven. Nirvana derives from the word meaning to waft away and according to one early Buddhist scripture:

> Nirvana is the area where there is no earth, water, fire and air; it is not the region of infinite space, nor that of infinite consciousness; it is not the region of nothing at all nor the border between distinguishing and not distinguishing; not this world nor the other world; where there is neither sun nor moon. I will not call it coming and going, nor standing still nor fading away nor beginning. It is without stopping. It is the end of suffering.

This gives a clear picture of what Nirvana is not, but what it is seems to be a misty picture built up from a list of things that it is not.

The fourth truth is where it begins to become further convoluted. This is the list of ways to remove suffering. Buddha made it into the Eightfold path; a set of eight rules that all good Buddhists should stick to and use as their talisman.

The first is Right Knowledge and understanding of the four noble truths.

The second is Right Attitude which involves a mental attitude of good-will, the removal of sensual desire, hate and malice.

The third is Right Speech. This means guarding every word and being wise, truthful and directed, rather than full of chatter, gossip and lies.

The fourth is Right Action embracing all moral behaviour, and demands a total rejection of murder, stealing and adultery.

Right Occupation is fifth on the path. It dictates that you must only pursue a job, or career, that does no harm to others.

The sixth is Right Effort; the suppression of evil impulses and the fostering of good intentions.

Right Mindfulness follows which entails consideration of all things, and the strength not to give in to desire in speech, thought, action or emotion.

The final fold of the path is Right Composure. This is achieved by intense concentration. This eighth code of conduct is supposed to free you from everything that holds you back in your quest for enlightenment.

We thought about the Eightfold path and made a few resolutions based on it, but they did not last for very long. The mounting tension of the climb did not act as a suitably calm oasis in which we could examine our beliefs, or play around with meditation and heavy breathing.

The remission was over and the rain returned. This time it was driving rain that we had to walk into all day. It never drew breath but pelted us in a persistent wall. Even the widowed Black hung in the protective wake of one of the porters, his sad tail, had he had one, would have hung between his legs, but instead his stub pointed downwards.

Our feeble array of rainwear came out again and Ella climbed back into her black plastic bag. A dense rain fog flopped into the valley, so that we could not see clearly, and the peaks around us disappeared into the damp.

Usually when faced with the ugly thought of a bad day's climbing there are practical things that you can focus on. There is the constant question of where your next foothold is going to be. This ends in frustration. You become so channelled into where you are next going to put your boot, you find yourself moving through exquisite landscapes without seeing anything but your feet and the rocks beneath them. The two day march from Tunda Buj to Bakh Bihar Tach was without this diversion; and a welcome preoccupation it would have been. It was just a long methodical climb over quite easy, wet ground. The only thing we had to look at was the gloom. The overriding priority was the vain attempt to keep any part of our bodies dry.

The first few hours of those days were the most depressing. Jane and I had discovered various ways of drying our clothes at night; socks and t-shirts were wrapped around our hot water bottles and underwear was put on our heads. The latter idea was based on vague memories of O-level Human Biology, and the lesson that most body heat was lost through the head.

Every night we sat in our sleeping bags with the hot water bottles wrapped in damp clothes at our feet and a variety of knickers on our heads. We tried to take pictures to make us laugh in the future, but the lenses clouded in condensation, giving our drying arrangements a vaguely raunchy appearance; a totally false impression, but it gave us hours of amusement.

We tried other ploys to forget the constant sound of rain on the tent. We talked about the years that we had both spent in Australia. The wetter our underwear was, the longer we had to talk to keep our brains alert, giving maximum heat radiation. We covered life in the bush and the memories of long days in the unrelenting dry heat; the joy of release from laced-up, county hunting to all-day rides in the outback; the seduction of the land personified by the recalcitrant, physical men with their nutty skin; those pretty poms, who gave up smart London to marry graziers, shipping their Colefax & Fowler lives out into the dust and the flies. We would fall asleep thinking about the heat, wondering what we were doing half way up a mountain in the pissing rain.

Our drying efforts meant that we started the day with partially dry and body warm underwear. It was the first hours, when those lovingly dried garments became soaked again, that were the worst. It was just another realisation of how pathetic our efforts were when pitched against the mountain.

After the initial soaking we were almost hypnotised by the need to keep going forward against the rain; just putting one foot in front of the other, and waiting for the next cold trickle of water to find one of the few warm crevices in our bodies. Each hour was marked off by one of us losing our temper for a while; a black moment when the rationale behind the whole expedition became absurd. In those dark commas of time everything became foul and far worse for you than for anyone else. You were the one who was wetter, colder, hungrier and more unhappy than anyone else could possibly be, or could understand. The worst of this passed away after a quick crossfire of abuse with whoever was nearest at hand. Black seemed to be the only one who was exempt from abuse, as we continued to respect his widower's weeds.

Will was in a downward spiral. He had not taken a picture since the hot springs at Khirganga because of the rain. The solo ranting in his tent was getting louder as he unpacked, patted, and repacked his cameras with increasing amounts of silicate. A couple of his lenses had started to fog, despite his efforts, and it made him increasingly dour and monosyllabic. He hung his head like Black's stub.

Jane shouted at the rain; when she woke up, as she walked, and as she went to bed. The other two girls tried to be Buddhist about it, but there were times when they looked at me with unbridled hatred as if I was in control of some great weather tap. I countered this with a thick layer of hockey field jollity. I chattered and played out cabaret turns when we stopped for breaks from our walk. Nobody laughed at me.

Jane and Ella had given up their efforts to stop smoking in the pure Himalayan air. So we now had an added minor drama with the battle to keep cigarette papers dry. They had started to barter their precious duty free packets with the porters in exchange for bidis, the tight tobacco rolled in ebony leaves that all the locals smoked. Bidis were milder than cigarettes and without as many of the chemicals. They also had a persistent habit of going out. This gave rise to a ritual of relighting behind sheltered rocks, in cupped hands, underneath dripping porter's blankets or our coats. Amanda occasionally succumbed when her Buddhism had worn thin.

Will seemed to find the whole tobacco saga quite amusing; and the constant struggle to light the bidis made him smile.

[62]

While dry matches had become the latest hard currency, an increasing sense of responsibility was becoming my main concern. As we spread out for each day's walk I found myself wrapped in a constant round of internal argument about the potential danger that I could be placing us in. My confidence was in flux. When we were all together I was becoming bluff. It gave a feeling of security and, even though it maddened the others, it meant that when decisions needed to be made my garrulous behaviour made me spokesman; a position where I would have to make decisions on gut reaction alone.

On the afternoon of this second day of walking in the heavy rain we stopped to shelter at the end of a long scrub pamir. There was a cove of high rock to protect us from the rain and the whole party flattened into the small area. Some of the porters shimmied up the rocks. They sat in a line above us on their haunches with rivulets of water running from the toes of their plastic shoes down the rock face. A cloud of steam filled the area. Nobody spoke and we clutched ourselves with our shoulders pulled up, and our heads retracted, tortoise-fashion, in an attempt to find some kind of warmth.

It seemed as if this was to be our next camp-site. It had been a long walk and we were not in the mood to head out into the rain again. The rocks we were sheltering under would be a safe haven for the cook tent. We began to take off our day packs, but none of the porters moved.

'Karma, are we going to camp here?'

He shrugged his shoulders at me and the rain dripped off his nose.

'No, half way now.' He took his backpack off and sat on it.

We moaned and looked out at the scrub, stretching away into the mist, and the grey wall of rain. One of the porters perched on the rock began to sing and the others joined him after the first few words. It could have been any song, none of us knew what they were singing about, but their tune was clear and bright, the verses punctuated with Gatling gun laughter. Their voices were clean in strange contrast to the hideous lung coughing from the porters' tent that filled each night.

It seemed as though the burst of song stopped at the point where the rain intruded into our shelter and that their tunes just filled our huddled space.

For a moment the sky took a breath and we moved out into the scrub again.

'I can smell hot chocolate.'

All I could smell was the wet earth and the acrid damp sweat from the porters.

[63]

'No, I'm wrong, it's soup, thick soup that makes your spoon move in slow motion.'

Jane was walking just behind me.

'I think you're wrong; it's fresh bread that has just been taken out of the oven and I'm going to burn my fingers tearing a piece off and putting butter on it.' She wiped a soggy glove across her face.

'A hot bath would be nice; so hot that all the mirrors would steam up.' Ella joined the fantasy.

'Stop it.' Amanda sounded as if she had caught a classroom of children with a dirty magazine. She strode on ahead, her plastic leggings swishing with authority against the scrub.

It had been a mental diversion that had been nipped in the bud and we resented it. There was an unattractive atmosphere, and we were heading for a verbal punch-up, when a strange, damp figure appeared at the back of the line of porters.

She seemed to have shrunk to about half her former height and her head hung down, almost perpendicular to the ground. She was soaking wet and limping badly, but, when she raised her head and realised that she was back with us, her tail came out from underneath her belly. There was a yelp from Black and he tumbled K Nau's bruised body in the scrub. The young bitch seemed to come back to life, barking and squirming.

The cloud broke up and the sun came through. The dogs frolicked like film stars and had a couple of failed attempts at sex. We reached the next camp-site at Bakh Bihar Tach. We washed our dirty clothes in a glacier stream, until our hands were numb, and Will celebrated K Nau's resurrection by washing himself and his worst socks.

The brightness was liquid sunshine, rather than a break in the weather, and the porters were once again pitching camp in the rain. It was the usual wet tents, damp sleeping bags, and piles of icy, partially clean underwear to wrap ourselves in.

Amanda and Ella were not happy. They retreated to their tent as soon as it had been pitched and did not come out of it when Karma produced the afternoon chai. Will, Jane and I sat in the cook tent, trying to decide whether we should drag them from their tent, to stop them from going into a vicious circle of self-analysis and unsuccessful meditation.

We drank chai and dunked biscuits until they were soggy and we came to no conclusion. We felt simple and uncomplicated; when we were wet, cold and low we could sit in front of a gas stove in the cook tent, drink tea, watch the dogs falling in love and feel better.

'Do you think it means that I'm very stupid that I don't have a major

View of Upper Mudh, Spiti Valley

Two novices sitting on the main stupa in the courtyard
of Tabo Gompa, Spiti Valley

A novice drawing Buddha on a geometrical grid
at Tabo Gompa, Spiti Valley

Children in a courtyard in Mudh looking up towards
the pass that we climbed over into the Spiti Valley

personality crisis when I get wet?' Will rescued his biscuit from his tea before it dissolved.

We just looked at him and said nothing. It made us laugh.

Karma was making chapattis, his dark fingers working the flour and water together deftly into a co-operative ball of dough. There was a curved metal plate over the fire in front of him. As the heat began to rise off the plate he plucked a small piece from the dough ball and rolled it in his palms. He threw the ball from palm to palm until it had flattened into a pancake, and then it was flicked onto the hot plate, left for a minute, and twitched over to brown the other side. As he worked he talked, and followed our conversation, the doughy slap of the chapattis against his palms punctuating his sentences. It was too wet to go outside so we had a go at chapatti making. After a long period of intense concentration we produced a few thick, inedible lumps that were grey and fingered. It made the guides laugh so much that Karma rocked backwards and forwards on his haunches like a demented monkey. We called out to Amanda and Ella to join the merriment, but there was silence from their tent.

Few emotional chasms are without reason and Ella's painful history, combined with her addictive nature, meant that all her battles were fiercer than the rest of ours. She twisted herself in and out of theoretical situations that did not even enter most of our minds. Her mother was suffering from advancing terminal throat cancer and a refusal to quit her heavy smoking. Ella carried this with her like a leaden ball and chain. She did not speak about it but it was always there in quiet moments. She was frightened of what she saw as her own weakness. Would she survive if she plunged over the cliff that she was trying to traverse? Would she faint if she looked down when she should be looking up? Would her body stand up to the test on the small amount of fuel that she was putting into it? All were questions that she grabbed hold of, and hung on to, in lurid detail, until they had played so many mental games with her that she could not see a simple way forward. The Buddhism was a balm but it had not got to the root of her complicated life.

Amanda's fears were harder to understand because there did not seem to be such straightforward scapegoats to pin her misgivings on. She was in a hiatus between being in control of her own little empire of classrooms and children, and what to do with her future. The Himalayas were a stage between the two but she seemed to be fighting any catalytic effect that they might have. The pictures that she created were angry sweeps of colour. She always made the landscapes seem more arid than they really were and there was usually a desolate figure, struggling to be seen, in the corner of the picture. It was hard for the chai-drinking simpletons to equate the lonely figure in the pictures with Amanda's tall, elegant body and measured voice.

Amanda and Ella had both found their way to a London Buddhist centre in the hope of finding something that they could utilise to rinse the muck out of their lives. Instead they found themselves up a wet mountain, trying to understand what they were looking for in the rain, while the non-Buddhists drank tea and failed to make chapattis.

Our disparate reasons for being in the Himalayas had led to a benign division in the party. Amanda and Ella were trying to make strides beyond the route into the Spiti Valley. They were searching each prayer flag for something more. To them, the *lap-tses* were not just mounds of stones on the top of passes, with animal horns and tatty washing lines of flags. They were trying to delve into the rural devotion that put the mounds of stones in place; mystical mounds that were another step for them up to the Buddhist baptism of Spiti.

Will and I saw piles of stones, lovingly heaped by local travellers across the high passes. We saw the skulls of animals and the curling, cracking horns. We saw the ragged pieces of material, frayed by the wind, the words of the prayers faded by the altitude. Will saw them in pictures and I saw them in words.

Jane had become a kind of go-between. When Will went to take his snaps (as all good photographers modestly insist on calling them) and I was wandering around the camp, talking to the porters or the guides, Ella and Amanda were hanging out at their spiritual station. Jane would slide into their tent and join in their circular, self-searching conversations. She would tell me if she felt they needed to have the security of Karma behind them as they walked, or if they were going to need a psychological boost.

While we played around with indecision and disillusion, the dogs were rising to the enormity of the landscape. Their reunion had finally broken down K Nau's flirty resistance. Perhaps her brush with death had made her see the errors of her cock-teasing. In a round of yelping and squawking Black finally managed to plant himself in the bitch. Her reaction was to spin onto her back underneath him with her rear end pulled off the ground by his suffering erection. Both of them ranted and K Nau struggled back onto her feet, but facing the wrong way. They had become genital Siamese twins.

They attempted to separate themselves and K Nau twisted onto her back again, but they ended up bottom to bottom once more. Somehow they staggered to the cook tent and stood looking at us with exhausted expressions, waiting for us to do something.

Will crossed his legs sympathetically. Jane was rolling a cigarette, and the guides were oblivious to the soap opera love story that we had set in motion.

Karma and the other guides, Sonam, Chetram and Tashi, had dragged large cooking pots of water back from the glacier streams to keep us supplied for that night. One of these pots was within my reach. It was not a gentle method of separation, but it was an effective one. They howled, parted and stood shaking and embarrassed as we laughed at them. This initial disaster did nothing to discourage them. So began a series of uncomfortable couplings.

We went to sleep to the sound of rain and woke to the same rhythm. According to the schedule that Paddy had drawn up for us we were due to have a rest day. There seemed to be little point in trying to move on in the pouring rain. It became an important day because, amidst all the frustration of being stuck in camp in the constant rain, we had come to the point where a decision had to be made.

As the others left the cook tent after breakfast Karma tapped my arm and signalled for me to stay. He had been watching Ella and Amanda during breakfast, obviously concerned by their withdrawal from camp life the previous afternoon. Ella had not eaten a proper breakfast. She had become slightly panicked when it was suggested that she should try and eat a bit more. She looked grey and tired and claimed not to have slept. Karma equated peace of mind with a healthy appetite. Neither Ella nor Amanda looked particularly robust that morning.

'We go back.' Karma looked at me expectantly.

It was hard to tell whether he was asking a question or giving me a piece of information. When it came to things of great importance his English deteriorated. His vocabulary was fluid when he was telling me a titbit about how the porters treated their wives or behaved when they got drunk, but when it came to drama he would shrug a lot, and prune his sentences to the barest minimum so that the meaning was often turned on its head.

'Why?' I asked assuming that he had given me a statement of fact rather than a question.

He looked at me, gave a big shrug and a half-hearted smile. He was worried about my leg, the physical and mental strength of Amanda and Ella, and the most important factor, he knew no more than we did about the territory that we were now going to enter.

Only one of the guides had been over the Pin Parvati La (pass) that led into the Pin and then the Spiti valley. Chetram had been over once before on a clear day in the sun, after several weeks of dry weather. Karma had been surprised by the difficulty of some of the climbing we had done so far. I had been fostering a secret since we left Manali.

Paddy had given me a revised version of the trek when we first arrived. Two things had leapt off the pages. The first, that we could not take pack ponies as originally planned because of the difficulty of the terrain; the second, that the climbing was difficult. Paddy's attitude to life meant that for him to admit that something was going to be difficult made it tantamount to impossible. I had edited the last page of the itinerary away into the bottom of the bag that I left in Manali. I had got away with it so far because the others had not seemed too concerned that the ponies had been replaced by men. Karma's expression reminded me of this economy with the truth.

'Very wet here, many snow up top for hard climbing.' He answered the question.

'What do the others think?' I asked.

Karma shrugged again. I looked at the other guides sitting in the gloomy morning light. They were crouched around the stove in an unenthusiastic fashion. I shrugged at them and they shrugged back. Sonam smiled, but it was a poor shadow of his usual bright expression. I tried to question them about what we might expect to encounter as we got higher, but none of them seemed to be able to do more than hazard a vague guess. Neither would they say that they thought it would be a good idea to turn back.

I left the cook tent an hour later having achieved nothing. The only time that turning back had crossed my mind was when my knee had gone at Khirganga. I had been treating the weather in Canute fashion, assuming that when we came to the pass the rain would dissolve into glorious sunshine. Karma had presented a new problem. I had not even asked the others about turning back, as it had not been a question in my mind, except immediately after the fall at the hot springs. Now it had crept in and with it came a trickle of panic; the idea that we would not get there, but would have to trail back through the mud and over the rock faces that we had seen before.

I was heading for Will's tent to air this new dilemma. Shribadur, the porter with the fur hat, ran across to me. He took my hand and pulled me towards the porters' tent. His grip was a surprise in the same way that I had been surprised when touching a snake for the first time, to find it dry and hoary rather than slithery.

The atmosphere in the tent was close to what it must have been like in the military bivouacs of Napoleon's unhappy army in Russia. There was the stink of discontent and poor health. Porters peered out from underneath layers of sodden blankets and frayed clothing. The overriding smells were of bad breath and stale sweat. Sick rose up my throat when I put my head through the front flap. Shribadur pulled me into the gloom towards two prone figures. They were both almost completely wrapped in blankets, clutching themselves in the foetal position.

They were the two that Ella and I had been rubbing with Vicks and feeding Disprins. Both of their faces were now like skulls, the skin sucked in from their high cheekbones. The man further from me was jammed into the corner of the dark tent so it was impossible to see him clearly. The second man was lying in the path of gloomy light from the tent flap. His eyes were rheumy and he seemed to find it difficult to focus. He tried to sit up when I squatted down beside him, but his arms were not strong enough to support his weight. Shribadur helped him to sit and he lolled against the fitter man's chest. He did not even have the strength to hold his head up. As he tried to look up his head flopped forward onto his chest, as if his spinal column had melted away, and left him like a dropped puppet.

'Hello.' I put my hand on his arm, but there seemed to be no flesh there, just bone.

As I touched him he managed to look up at me blindly and put his hand to his chest. He took a shallow breath. It rattled through him and he began to cough; great sucking hacks that trapped his whole body and then dropped it back into the blankets. He put his hand to his mouth and then showed it to me, his shaking palm outstretched. It was covered in black, congealed lumps that could have been balls of smoker's tar from his lungs. It took me a few moments to realise that it was clotted blood and lung wall.

'Christ, he's got TB.' I turned to Shribadur in horror as I realised that every one of those sick porters was suffering from various degrees of tuberculosis. I could smell the blood that this man was coughing up.

Shribadur flicked his head from side to side in acknowledgement. He looked at me, waiting for me to do something for the dying man.

Tales of TB filtered back, the highly contagious nature of the disease, the ways the bacteria were passed through the air, via close contact with the clothing, food and bodies of the victims. It shocked me to be face to face with a disease that is so rarely heard of in Europe, even though about 12 000 cases are reported each year in Britain. To the porters it was a common part of their daily lives, a disease that they carried on working with until it killed them.

One of my first reactions was anger. This man had been employed on a trek where he was going to be shoulder to shoulder with other men whom he was going to infect with the disease. I could not believe that it had not been obvious to the guides employing him that they were taking an uncalculated risk in sending out a man who was going to suffer in the damp, and have the tuberculosis accelerated by the high altitude as increasing pressure was put on his weakening lungs. There was little point in overreacting and I was aware that there would be a reason behind it all.

The story of the Nepalese porters unfolded slowly. The Manali guides looked down on them as inferior work animals. They treated them fairly, but they made sure that the porters were always camped well away from the rest of us, and there was rarely any traffic between their tent and the cook tent.

These Sherpas come down from Nepal in great packs during the trekking season to earn money to carry them through the winter months. The intention of saving any money usually dissipates with the first cash they receive. As with so many of the tribal people of the world, these wiry men, who originated from Tibet, seem to be more poisoned by alcohol than the rest of us. They take their drinking and gambling very seriously. If they have lost their shirt and are doused in arak (a potent, illegal brew that ploughs your throat with distilled barley), they would rather sleep in an open sewer than waste their gambling money on a bed for the night. This was the picture that our guides painted of these men. They felt that they had low moral standards and even lower levels of hygiene; and that by whooping it up around the gambling tables and sleeping rough in the damp Himachal climate the Sherpas laid themselves open to the tuberculosis bacteria. In fact one of the major causes of the disease is a nasty invader called M. Bovis that thrives on dairy products. It is now almost unknown in the West because of the effectiveness of pasteurisation, but in this part of the Himalayas pasteurisation is almost unheard of. We stuck to dried milk and imported processed cheese, but the Sherpas drank local milk and ate cheese and curd while they were down in Manali. For some indigenous reason they have a low tolerance to the disease, so it is a dangerous predator amongst the immigrant porters. It is not hard to understand why the people of Manali shun them. They see it as a way of protecting their vulnerable children, and themselves, against the disease. It seems sadly ironic that it is this disease that kills these high altitude people when one of the cures in the past was to send sufferers into clean mountain air.

My whole body had gone into a subconscious recoil when I had realized that it was TB. The BCG jab at school seemed too remote to be an effective deterrent now. I remembered terrible Victorian engravings of children, with metal cages around their chests to support their lungs, and the stories of pained consumptives dying slowly beside Swiss lakes. Jangrabadur, one of the older porters, was standing right behind me, his leg stopping me from moving away from the suffering man. As the closer man stopped coughing the other one started. The first man wiped the blood off his hand onto his blanket and slumped back against Shribadur.

'Is he eating?' I asked Shribadur.

'Kilo rice one day.' He pointed to a bowl beside the man and raised three fingers to show his daily consumption. It was hard to believe that this shadow of a man could eat so much and still continue to lose weight dramatically. Karma sometimes complained about the amount of rations that the porters got through, claiming that over half the porters were just carrying the food for themselves. It made sense now; people with tuberculosis often have an increase in appetite paralleled by a loss of weight.

We had a small supply of antibiotics with us, but they were very general ones for the treatment of flesh wounds and cases of dysentery. I had no idea whether they would be appropriate for treating TB. Rest, good food, a break from all physical activity and the removal of any stress were the traditional cures. There was slim chance of either of these men getting this supportive attention; their food was very basic and not very nutritious, their living conditions were squalid, they were re-infecting themselves on a daily basis because of the lack of hygiene, and it was almost impossible to rest with the coughing that filled their tent all the time. The constant rain and the increasing altitude were red rags to this disease as well as adding bronchitis to the victims' pathetic immune systems.

I realised how conspicuously useless I was being, crouched in front of this sick man, thinking on my haunches.

'Could I see his chest?' I made an undressing gesture.

Shribadur shrugged and unwrapped the blankets from around the man.

'Yama, Yama,' Jangrabadur was still behind me, mumbling.

'Yama?' I pointed at the sick man, assuming that this was his name.

Shribadur shook his head violently and drew his hand across his throat gesturing that I should shut up. I found out later that Yama is the Nepalese god of death. Oribadur was the name of the man I had been brought to help.

His ribs were riding close under his skin as he tried to breathe in short, shallow breaths, and a delta of blue veins showed through his skin around his sternum. The last time I had rubbed him with Vicks he had felt fragile and brittle but now he was a character from Belsen, his body hardly recognisable as the human form that we are familiar with. I placed my hands on the front and back of his chest and waited for him to breathe again. It must have been humiliating for him to have me touching him in such a pitiful state. He started to cough again at the contact of my hands. This time the blood shot straight out of his mouth and splattered against Jangrabadur's pale grey trouser leg. Now the blood was bright red; almost orange in the weak light.

'You must keep him upright, he will find it easier to breathe.' I signalled to Shribadur to prop Oribadur and the other sick man up.

'We need some dry blankets for them and you must make sure that their plates are kept away from the rest. They need to be kept warm and they need sleep and food. You must not let the blood that they cough out touch you and you must burn this blanket.' My voice was rising as I pointed to the bloodstained blanket that Oribadur was wrapped in.

'I am going to talk to Karma about this.' I got up and looked around at the rest of the porters. They were all looking at me as if I was the fluffy bit on a game show. I backed out of the tent and ran back to the cook tent.

Karma was still making chapattis for the day, his hands slapping to the rhythm of the dough. I sat down beside him.

'Chai Mem?' Karma had a habit of calling me 'Mem' when he thought that I was about to ask him to do something. He had read the expression on my face.

'No tea thanks, but I need to talk to you about the porters. Did you know that some of them are very ill with tuberculosis?' Karma gave me the Indian head wobble and turned his attention back to his chapattis.

'I think one of them may die if he does not get rest, good food and dry blankets. He is infecting the others all the time. He coughs blood all over them and he is lying, wrapped in a damp blanket, on the wet ground.' I was waving my hands around, trying to convey the enormity of the problem.

Karma carefully placed the chapatti that he had been making onto the flour-covered tin that he was working over.

'They eating very much rice each day. Each one of them eat the same rice as three of you. We will be running out before many days.' He wiped his face with his floury hand turning it into a dusted granary bap.

'The rice is not good enough for sick men.'

'Rice is good enough for you.' Karma sounded irritated.

'We're not ill Karma.' This was not how I had planned the conversation to run.

He picked up the chapatti and threw it onto the hot plate. I was being short-sighted and making Karma's job even harder, but I did not want to have a dead man on the trek. To Karma, TB is a common disease that he comes into contact with on a daily basis. He would have known that he had a very high chance of having a few porters, who might have seemed quite healthy down in Manali, but who would prove, during the trek, to be suffering from the disease. It was to be expected.

'We go back?' That was the second time in one morning, but this time Karma was presenting it to me as a challenge.

I kicked one of the battered cooking pots at my feet and it clattered against several others. Sonam and Chetram ran into the tent, assuming that Karma was in the throes of kitchen violence. They retreated when they saw who the protagonist was. Karma plucked another piece of dough and began the methodical flattening process. I was standing uncomfortably over him amidst the disarray of cooking pots. He finished the chapatti and pulled off another piece of dough. He held it out to me and motioned for me to sit down. The other guides stopped hovering outside the tent and came back in.

'What can we do?' I kneaded the small ball in my hand.

Sonam and Chetram looked at Karma, unsure of what we were talking about.

'Sometime it their game so no more carrying for sick man,' he said.

'Come on, you can't fake lumps of your lungs coming up.'

They all looked bemused. They did not understand what I had said.

'Oribadur is very ill. I think he will die if he goes on.'

Sonam smiled as I spoke. 'Not dead if not to carry and he go slowing.' He shuffled across to Karma remaining in his squat as he moved.

Chetram settled next to Sonam so that they were a united front.

'Well, if the weather goes on like this, we will probably have to go back anyway.' It came out before it had been thought through. It was the first spoken admission that there was doubt in my mind.

Both of my fists were clenched. Karma took one of my hands and uncurled the fingers.

'Still no good for chapatti.' He extracted the little grey ball of sticky dough from my palm and grinned.

No one knew what we should do. We talked about it and came to no conclusion as we had no practical facts to base a decision on. We sat in a cross-legged circle and played cards. There was shouting when Ella was slow to pick up the rules. Will sat at the outer edge of the circle making no effort to hide the fact that he was picking his toenails. Jane won and the rest of us were poor losers.

Karma turned to comfort feeding. Lunch appeared as the cards were becoming dangerous. Sonam, Chetram, Tashi and Karma came in a procession, each bearing the ingredients of our lunch: a large pile of freshly made chapattis in a surprisingly clean cloth, a bowl of ladies' fingers, brewed up with sweet chillies, a carefully arranged cheese, tomato and onion salad, even the dull *dhal* had been dressed in party clothes with pulses and onions. Karma had dug deep into the food reserves to try and lighten the mood.

The spices in the Indian diet are deliberately balanced to suit, enliven or improve the mood of the eater. The different uses of chilli combat the four Chaucerian Humours; temperament of mind, state of mind, disposition and caprice. If ever you are in India in a foul frame of mind, some wise matriarch will prescribe a dinner of elaborate masalas to combat your temper. The strength of some of the spices is enough to occupy your wrath, but, like Japanese food, the Indian diet is based on a rule of combining ingredients to enhance the quality of life. If you stick to the Indian staples, based around rice and vegetables, your body does start to function to a higher standard, once it has got used to the blast of the spices. These alone act as purifiers in the gut.

It is the Indian sweet tooth that has upset the balance of their basic regime. You need only spend a few minutes in one of their sweet shops during a festival to discover their total lack of self control when it comes to sugar.

Will and I had once been caught in a sweet stampede. We had been photographing the shops of Delhi for an exoteric guide to beating Conran by buying direct in the Indian capital. We had been advised to get to the sweet market early to see the shops fully stocked at the start of the day.

We alighted from a rickshaw a few minutes before opening time in the Bengali Sweet Market near Connaught Place. The shops are clutched around in a small circle and that morning the street outside was empty except for an orange juice boy. He was crushing some oranges in a press fixed to the back of his bicycle. When he had a full glass he scurried across the road and gave the glass to the owner of Nathus, one of the most popular shops in the market. The man flicked the boy away with a coin. The lad went back to his bicycle and climbed on, settling his back against the seat, as he was too small to sit on it. The shopkeeper was already sweating, even though it was still the morning cool. He was shouting at the counter boys as they laid out trays of sweets in creamy rows, some flecked with gold and silver, or dotted with nuts and chocolate. There were trays of flaky Barfi, made from evaporated milk and sugar and flavoured with pistachios; Karachi Halwa, the chunks of glistening, sweet marrow marinated in sugar; Patisa, a mixture of chickpea flour, ghee and sugar; Jelabis, K Nau's weakness, the coils of light batter, deep-fried and soaked in syrup; Gulab Jamun, again evaporated milk and sugar, this time fried and soaked in honey syrup; Chum Chums, the ovals of desiccated coconut, some filled with fluffy mallai cream; Pati and Chiky, the raw sugar known as jaggery, flavoured with cashews and pistachios, giving it a similar flavour and texture to Turkish Delight. At the back of the shop were large, shining containers of Kulfi, the famous Indian ice-cream, sitting on fat blocks of ice, the size of benches. In front of the counter was a spread of empty tables and chairs. A boy in a grey cotton suit, with Nathus emblazoned across his back, was taking the chairs down. The owner carried his large belly from behind the counter. He spat into the palms of his hands and smoothed his sparse hair back over his shining pate. He grabbed the boy and did the same thing to him. It was opening time.

We had been standing in the quiet street watching the action in the shops. The stillness evaporated into a bustle of shouting, shifting bodies as the sweet shops opened their doors. In the space of five minutes the circle of shops was full of householders buying up for Dussehra, the important Hindu festival celebrating Rama's victory over the demon king, Ravana. We knew the ten day celebration culminates in the burning of effigies, when the Ganges becomes clogged with flaming figures of Ravana and Rama, their straw limbs pitched in combat. What we had not realised was that it also calls for an orgy of sweet eating, as do all festivals in India.

Every heavy-chested and fisted Delhi dowager seemed to have descended on the Bengali Sweet Market in those five minutes. Chubby fingers were reaching out across the counters to try and grab the attention of the rushing counter boys. The same fingers were plucking samples from the trays and most of the ordering was made through mouths full of Barfi and Chum Chums. Small children were jostling the overhanging trays to try and knock sweets off the edge and into their hands.

The women of Delhi seem to weigh their social importance by the size of the boxes that they carry home from the sweet market. Some of these boxes, leaving the market in front of us, were almost beyond vulgarity in size. They were often too big for the women to carry, so rickshaw wallahs were summoned from their vehicles to carry away the booty.

Some were too impatient to wait until they got home. They spread themselves over the tables and chairs, consuming plates of sweets and small cups of coffee with darting fingers and eyes. Only the quicker-witted children had a share of the pickings.

We left at the end of this rush hour, shell-shocked and carrying only a very small box from Nathus that we had bought from an exhausted counter boy with a fixed smile.

Karma had not been able to produce Jelabis and Kulfi for us in the rain, but he succeeded in filling us up from the rations and taking our minds off the decision making process.

The weather was flirting with us. We peered out of the tent after lunch and some of the mist had rolled away. We could see the outline of the sun through a thin layer of sprinting cloud. We emerged stretching, and disappeared behind various rocks. Karma came out of the cook tent smiling. There seemed to be a note of optimism. Stooped figures appeared from the porters' tent, unfolding themselves in the light. I asked Karma to come to the porters' tent. He followed me with a lack of enthusiasm.

There was a crouched figure in front of the tent and he signalled that Shribadur was to our left. The fur-hatted porter had his back to us and he was peeing down wind so that the yellow arc was carried away from him. Black was next to him, having less success with the wind and showering his belly.

I waved at Shribadur as he turned back to us, and he waved back, unabashed as he readjusted himself. Karma muttered behind me.

'How is Oribadur?' I asked.

'Same, same.' Shribadur pointed into the tent.

We went in and found the two porters lying as they had been earlier. I had some Disprin and a glass of water with me. Oribadur was asleep and his breathing sounded easier. The second porter took two Disprins, holding onto my arm as he swallowed them.

Karma and Shribadur had a rapid conversation. It was hard to ascertain what they were talking about. Their sentences were clipped and both of their faces were bland. Karma left the tent and I trotted after him, leaving the rest of the Disprin, and the glass of water next to Oribadur. They were probably useless but it was something visible that might encourage his psyche.

'What did Shribadur say?' I asked Karma.

'He say if you going, they going, if you going back, they going back.' He did not look at me as he spoke, and I doubt it was the conversation that they really had.

'What do you think?'

'Maybe clearing, maybe not.' He returned to the cook tent and I went back to the second round of cards as the rain began again.

The monotony was broken by the appearance of Sonam's smile through the tent flap with a large pot of chai and a tray of freshly made popcorn. We descended on it and hardly noticed that the top layer had been softened by the rain.

'If the rain goes on we may not be able to get up to the pass.' It was the first time that I had broached the subject directly amongst the five of us.

'Will we have to go back?' Ella asked.

'I hope not.' I looked to Will for some support, but he was silent.

'How's your leg?' Jane knew that it was still hurting me because she heard me groaning in and out of my sleeping bag.

'It's fine,' I snapped.

'Oh really?' Her tone was sarcastic.

'I don't want to climb back down those rocks,' Ella said.

'I don't want to have to go back at all.' I turned to Will again but he was having his neck massaged by Ella and his eyes were closed.

'We should go on if we can. It would be such a waste to have got to here and not try.' I tried to sound determined.

'I think we should go on.' Amanda surprised me and I was delighted.

Jane got up and left the tent. She came back a minute later.

'It's stopped raining again.' She said and left.

Jane was angry and felt that I was being irresponsible in insisting on continuing without the practical knowledge and equipment that we might need. She was right, but I was not going to admit that then.

We went outside to take advantage of the latest respite.

A curious figure was making its way down the valley towards us. As it came closer we could make out the distinctive form of a sadhu. His matted hair was coiled on the back of his head and his beard covered the upper part of his chest. It was the only protection that his body had apart from the loincloth hanging from his hip bones. He was barefoot, carrying only a staff, with his alms bowl around his neck, bumping off his chest as he walked.

As he came into the camp he gave a munificent smile. His eyes had the same watery expression of all the sadhus. He stood amongst us, his body smooth against the cold wind, while we hung around him in thick layers and expensive fleeces. He was standing on one leg, in a Yoga pose, with his other foot pressed hard into the upper thigh of his standing leg.

Sonam was talking to him in Hindi, asking him where he had come down from and what the conditions were like higher up.

The sadhu threw his hands up in the air and rolled his eyes. He had just come down from Mantalai, the place where we were planning to make our next camp, and the last stop before the glacier on the way up to the pass. He had turned back because of the weather. We looked at his bare feet. He saw our expressions and laughed at us.

Karma told him that we were planning to go on up to the pass if the rain stopped. The sadhu danced around us, spinning his staff like a drum majorette and cackling with laughter. He stopped his jig in mid hop and resumed his one-legged pose. His expression was serious, and, for a moment, his eyes focused. He told us not to go on to Mantalai.

Ella and Jane were in their tents so they did not hear the prophet of doom. I told Will and Amanda that the sadhu had said that it was snowing up on the top, but that he had just been over the pass. They probably knew that I was lying, but they did not challenge me.

When I got back to the tent Jane was writing her diary, digging deep into the pages and dripping them with vitriol at my cost. I draped a substantial pair of knickers on my head but it did not make her laugh. It made her more angry that I was trying to ingratiate myself whilst playing Russian Roulette with our lives.

The rain was, once again, rattling on the tent, but for once it did not carry the aura of despondency with it. I had become instilled with a sense of urgency that we must go on and try to get up to the glacier, despite the rain, so that we were in the right place to have a go at the pass before the snow got too deep.

Going back was no longer an option. Oribadur's bloodstained blanket had made it a momentary certainty, until it had become apparent that virulent tuberculosis was something that the guides expected on the journey.

The danger in combining travel and youth is the strong feeling of immortality that the latter carries. When there is a disaster this results in a diminished sense of responsibility. It did not seem possible that we could face this kind of drama. The idea of going back on our tracks seemed so pedestrian, as if we had been caught in the rain on a Sunday afternoon stroll and did not want to get wet. The taste of adventure and the flirtation with leadership had warped my logic. The practical blacklist of accidents were things that would be faced and surmounted if they happened, but I had not planned for them.

I slept with a mounting excitement that we were now stepping into the realms of the explorer and beyond the labelling of tourist and trekker.

From the following day onwards the porters formed a splinter group. The majority of them stayed just behind the guides and our group of five. At an increasing distance behind, Oribadur and the second sick porter were intermittently carried and supported by two other porters. The latter two were not exactly robust characters. Karma had chosen them on the premise that they probably had TB so at least they could not be newly infected. This motley crew carried a bivouac and rations for the four of them to survive on in case either of the really sick men became too ill to move, so separating them from our main group for a night. There seemed to be a vague plan to cover this eventuality: if they were left behind another porter from our group would go back to find them, and from there go on back for help. This plan was roughly translated to me on the morning that we set off for Mantalai. Chetram found it difficult to convey the message. He spoke Pahari with a thick accent and it meant that I understood only about one in fifty words. Most of it came across in mime. Karma had sent him across to give me the message about the porters. He was becoming sharp about using a go-between when he did not want to be questioned about something. Trying to understand the verbal contortions, and the red herrings that they threw up, was more than enough to divert me from any line of questioning.

The rain began to freeze as we got higher and we came into Mantalai with our breath hanging in the air as icy puffs. We made our camp on a rise above the valley floor away from the dumping ground at the foot of the glacier where the ice spat out the rocks that it had swallowed in its path. It was not a pretty place; more a motorway building site than a natural valley floor, as though huge dumper trucks had gashed through the landscape and left behind piles of rubble and silt. Some of it was still in jagged lumps of ice, scattered like bombed buildings, where the glacier had spat them out, others were just rubbish piles of grey mud and rock. It was bleak and cold.

Jane I sat in our tent with pages of *The Economist* wrapped around our feet to dry them out and warm them. Jane only had her track shoes, and their lack of insulation against the wet and cold was beginning to split the skin on her feet. There was no longer any vanity. We had no mirrors and no audience. We no longer went to the cook tent in search of conversation when the mood suited us, but out of a need for warmth.

Our little group had changed from the wary five who had met up under neon lights in the airport check-in a few weeks before. Will was slumped under Ella's thumbs as she massaged him. He grunted at cogent points of her explanations of the powers of meditation. Amanda had succumbed to a headache, exacerbated by lurid details of the early warning signals of AMS (Acute Mountain Sickness or terminal altitude sickness). Jane and I had fallen into helpless laughter after a protracted argument about who should have the last bit of sock-drying space on the side of a half full, half cold kettle.

Until this point in our journey we had all moved and functioned as separate piece that did not want to fit together. Now that we were so far removed from the daily comforts of our own disparate lives we had slowly begun to cohere. The terrifying flood reports that came through on Will's radio, of the thousands dying in Pakistan, made our position seem even more fragile. The need for familiar security made our voices, and even our moanings, resound with a comforting note. Even though it was still raining there had been no mention of going back. There was a feeling of nerves and laughter, the slightly heightened sense of drama that comes before a test with any kind of risk attached to it. Our adrenalin was taking over.

I woke in the middle of the night with the sound of pounding in my ears. I just managed to get my head out of the tent before I was sicker than I had been since those painful days of car sickness as a child. I got out of the tent and stood shivering on the plateau of ground outside. The rubble of the glacier was casting shadows across the ground below. It was a bright night and no clouds passed in front of the moon. There was no rain, only the bitter cold and the white moon. It picked out the crags and shattered edges of the valley sides. The nausea grabbed me again and I crawled back into the tent feeling weak and scared by the thought of trying to climb. I was too frightened to sleep in case the sickness was a symptom of altitude sickness. I lay and willed the morning to come when the dark pangs of the night would be pushed aside by the sound of Karma's voice waking us with bed tea. Giardia is a foul-mouthed parasite that hangs around in contaminated water. It can lurk in your gut for several weeks, or it can set to work immediately causing stomach cramps, nausea, vomiting, a bloated stomach, stinking diarrhoea and noxious gas that makes it almost impossible for anyone else to survive in close proximity to a sufferer. The giardia parasite ignores antibiotics and thrives, in clouds of green gas, on any food that you put into your body.

The sun was shining out of a cold blue sky the following morning. I sat on a rock waiting for the warmth to comfort my giardia. My humiliation was completed by Jane's loud complaints about the constant stench that I had around me and by the dogs' voracious consumption of my vomit. I did not even have the energy to move away from the scene of their foul feast.

Karma had the answer. I must not eat, but just drink freshly boiled water with lemon. This, he assured me, would starve out the parasite. So I drank boiled water at breakfast and put my trust in Karma.

That one sleepless night had given me an idea of how much Ella suffered when she could not get to sleep night after night. There is a strange hatred that builds up in an insomniac when their bedfellow lolls in deep sleep while they rant at the night. I could see the jealousy in Ella's eyes when I used to answer about how well and deeply I had slept. I have heard insomniacs talking about the cruel characters that stalk the stage during their sleepless nights. These must have been multiplied by the hallucinogenic nature of thin air. The dark rings around her eyes were just another testament to the fact that she was finding everything a little harder than the rest of us, yet she always spoke the first words of sympathy whenever any of the rest of us had something wrong.

Whatever our domestic problems, nothing could detract from the fact that we were basking in uninterrupted sunshine for the first time since we had set out.

It took a long time to pack up the camp. I was useless and could not even get to the porters' tent to see if Oribadur's party had caught up the previous night. We set off towards the glacier but it was not a good start. We had to take off our boots to cross a glacier stream just as we left camp. Jane lost her sense of humour. She hates having to walk through water with bare feet, and this, combined with her split skin, made her howl as we crossed. But whilst it made Jane miserable it was an effective stimulant for me. It was an electric shock to the system although the afterglow did not last long enough.

We started the day climbing over the boulders and lumps thrown out by the glacier. It was slow progress and it suited me. I hung as far back as I could to keep out of everyone else's range of smell and to give myself rests after each stretch of clambering. This did not last as we turned left out of the valley bottom to face the almost vertical mountain wall. There

[81]

was no option but to start climbing. It was a matter of minutes before we were strung out across the steep valley side.

I could see Will and Jane right up at the front with Chetram and Karma. I had managed to persuade Karma to go on ahead rather than linger with me and my vile gases. It was not a decision that I remained happy with as the day progressed.

The porters passed me almost before I had started to climb. There was a long interval and then the TB party came past without Oribadur. I could see him further down the incline, huddled on a piece of jutting rock, with his blanket cocooned around him. We were the flotsam at the rear. Each time I looked up I could see the others pulling further away up the climb, and each small patch that I covered seemed to become harder. I could hear Oribadur's breathing below, rasping and painful, but the sound of my own almost drowned his out. I was trying to establish why I was so weak. I knew that I was vulnerable because of the giardia attack, but the way it had sucked every ounce of energy out shocked me. For every step that I climbed up I would have to wait to recover, panting and hanging on to the edge of the valley, clinging to tufts of vegetation or the edges of rocks. It was a mistake to keep looking up. If I had watched the painful progress of the man below me, rather than the healthy ascent above, I might not have become so pathetic. He was dying, and yet he was managing to climb, and all I had was a parasite and an ill wind.

The most frightening thing about the climb was that the parasite made me lose my sense of balance. To fall would have been final. There was nothing that would stop a body before hitting the bottom and joining with the other detritus from the glacier.

In the middle of the climb there was a section of fine, loose scree that ran away from my foothold as soon as I had planted my boot. I was trying to cross from one gully into another where I had seen the others climb up with relative ease. I leant forward to take a large stride across the gully and the valley side spun around me. As I felt myself falling I could not remember seeing anything that I could grab hold of. The only thing that seemed to be important was that I did not fall on top of Oribadur. I dug my fingers into the scree and I found a root under the surface. It stopped me, and I lay gasping across the rise of the gully side. My heavy breathing turned to sobbing, great gulps of relief that poured out of me followed by a tirade of abuse directed at the others for not being there. I swore at Karma for not being with me when I really needed him. But the shock and anger subsided into laughter. He had simply followed a man's logic and done what a woman had asked him to do without searching for a second meaning. I could not be that ill if I could swear, cry and laugh. Below me Oribadur made no sound except for the harsh rhythm of his breathing.

I stopped looking up for the rest of the climb, and just counted ten paces at a time followed by a minute of rest. The valley side finally sank away below me and I reached the top. Karma was waiting, sitting on a rock in the sun, smiling at me as I struggled over the top lip of the valley wall. I had lost track of time, so I did not know how long they had been waiting there. They clapped when I appeared and it filled me with a sense of achievement. It also gave me another burst of energy to make the last walk to Camp One below the pass. In the thrill of the moment I forgot about Oribadur, still on the valley wall fighting his way to the top. I did not hear about him until the next day, the longest day.

6

A HIGH PASS

T HE stones around us sparkled, fool's gold waiting to be gathered up and to weigh us down. At sunset, after the long climb to Camp One, it began to snow and the silvery flakes settled on the stones around our tent in a glittering, frozen landscape.

Once the sun had gone it was too cold to be out of a tent for more than a couple of minutes. We did not have Antarctic clothing to stride around in, so bodily warmth was a valuable commodity that we had to protect. We ran from tent to tent in short bursts.

Supper was even earlier than usual, as it was too cold to sit around in the cook tent watching Karma perform with the gas stoves. The others ate and I talked, trying to fill the hole in my stomach with boiling water, lemon and inane conversation. So I talked and planned and told the shaggy-dog story of how it is never supposed to rain in the Spiti Valley, because the clouds cannot get over the Pin Parvati peaks that border the valley. I was confident about the next day as nothing could be worse than that climb up to Camp One. The thought of a night of real sleep also helped curb the hunger. I had been looking forward to that first moment of contact with the sleeping bag from the sound of Karma's voice with bed tea that morning. I knew I would sleep through sheer exhaustion, but it was not going to be a good night for everyone. While Jane and I lay in deep sleep, the others were suffering from the increased height and misgivings about the following day. Amanda woke several times in the night, her body jerking her awake as it began to struggle for oxygen. Ella and Will just missed out on sleep altogether.

The day began with bright sun, sheet white off the layer of snow, and frost around the tents. The warmth cut through the early freeze within half an hour of appearing from behind the surrounding peaks. It was the first time that we had seen a clear view from the camp. Above us was a swoop of smooth glacier running down from the pass in a clean tumble. The rest was a 270 degree spread of the peaks of the Himalayas, each one decked in white and sparring with its neighbour to pierce the clouds. That was all we could see, a horizon of summits laid out around us in a carpet of spearheads.

The world becomes very large when you are sitting on the roof of it. You are so far above the minutiae of daily life. It is easy to understand why mountain people find cities so terrifying; the rush, the haze of pollution, the solid queues of tiny people in metal boxes, jammed together in battle with the changing traffic lights. The silence and space of the High Himalayas throws your world into bright perspective. It is very levelling to realise your own size in the face of such enormity. There have been so many fluid and elegant descriptions of the glory of mountains, but these giants are like most things; there are those who are passionate about them, while others are left cold by the idea of climbing boots and high altitude. Even if they do not inspire you, some deference must be shown to the overwhelming power of the earth to throw up these 'age old sentinels of time' as Jawaharlal Nehru referred to them.

Will and his camera came back to life. The layers of silicate were thrown aside and the lenses extracted from their loving storage. He ran around the camp as the porters picked up our tents and shook the snow and frost from them. He caught them as the dusting of ice sprinkled down around them, flashed by the sun. He jumped on to rocks and squatted in hollows to try and capture the unending sweep of peaks around us. He ordered us away from our tents to try and photograph the passing effect of our empty temporary homes, miniaturised by the horizon behind. His whole body seemed to have been changed and revitalised by purpose. He was upright and agile as he danced around us, issuing orders, and partnering his tripod, as he waltzed between rocks and tents. For the first time he set out for the day with a camera around his neck, rather than hunched miserably under his backpack loaded with sealed camera cases.

Karma had insinuated that the climb over the pass would be one of our longest days, but he had the foresight not to go into details, or actual time estimates; the vital number of hours' climbing that we were always trying to extract from him.

As on every other day, we set off before the porters, but when I looked over my shoulder, as we started to climb into the snow, I saw them hurrying to leave camp and catch up with us. It meant nothing to us then.

We headed straight up the glacier that rolled into Camp One. It was covered in about a foot of powder snow that flew up in feathery puffs as we flicked it off our boots with each step. It was a gentle climb and the sun was a novelty that gave us all an injection of confidence. We jumped and kicked at the powder, sending it up in clouds and watching the rainbows that it made as it caught the sun. K Nau and Black bounced in the snow. They jumped, rolled, growled at it and bit into it, sneezing as the powdery flakes rushed up their noses. Even the guides seemed enthused by the escape from the rain.

Chetram and Sonam were puppy-fighting in the snow until the fluff had covered them in a white coating and they too began to sneeze. They got up like two little boys, giggling and jostling. Sonam wiped the snow from his face with the tail of his shirt and wrapped his scarf around, just below his eyes. He cleaned his sunglasses and put them back on, pulling his baseball cap down over the only other exposed skin. Chetram took his glasses off and ran them through the snow. When he put them back on they were still covered in a layer of snow. He took them off and put them in his pocket.

We came to the point on the glacier where it ran away from the curve of the mountainside. Karma grabbed both of the dogs and pushed them across towards the snow field on the mountain. K Nau sank in, right up to her belly, but Black seemed to have found lighter snow. Karma led us across in Black's path. One of my legs shot down into the snow and seemed to go through into air. After we had crossed, we looked back to see that we had just come over a narrow ice bridge spanning the wide gap between the glacier and the mountainside. My leg had gone over the edge of the bridge and into the void below. K Nau had managed to run across the drift of snow between; her lightness had stopped her from falling through into the crevasse.

The porters knew to follow in our footsteps. We stood above the glacier and watched them thread their way across the bridge, a dotted line of ants picking their way through the snow in their sockless, plastic shoes. The sun reflected blue off the white landscape, throwing them into silhouette.

We sat on the lip of the snow field waiting for the porters to finish crossing the ice bridge. We had sun, height and virgin snow. The rest of the world seemed to have receded. For the first time I felt that I had made the right decision to carry on. It was elating.

Karma was sitting on a rock hunched up like a vulture. It was difficult to see where he was looking because of the black mask of his sunglasses, but I was on a level with him so I could see behind the lenses. He was gazing around with the same awe as we were. It was all as new to him as it was to us.

Will was standing above Karma.

'Which way is the pass?' He directed his question at Chetram and Karma.

Karma shrugged and passed the buck to Chetram, who had his head bent into his lap and was rubbing his eyes.

'Which way is it, Chetram?' I asked the bowed figure.

He did not lift his head from his lap, but waved his hand in the direction that went straight up the snow field.

So we began to climb.

The snow was getting thicker and it was heavier than the powder had been down on the glacier. It coated our legs and soaked them. The dogs were beginning to suffer from the altitude, but they did not understand it. As their muscles ran out of oxygen they collapsed in the snow and lay, limp and panting, until they felt strong enough to get up again. When they tried to run they just flopped down and lay heaving.

Will was shouting at himself and the snow. He kept losing his sense of balance and staggering as he climbed. In contrast, I was not the same human being who had sworn her way up the glacier wall the day before. I had a surge of energy. Karma was adamant that this had been released by the day of fasting and that I was reaping the benefits of the physical practices of Buddhism. Whatever the reason was, I could feel the adrenalin racing the red and white corpuscles around my body. The old news footage of Neil Armstrong, drifting in liquid motion across the moon, came to mind as my strides seemed to have a floating ease.

We moved methodically in the footsteps made by the person in front. The guides took it in turns to lead because it meant making the first impressions in the deep snow. It was hard work and after about half an hour they would drop further back in the line, panting and sweating, and allow someone else to take over. Chetram was never at the front and he seemed to be dropping further back each time we stopped for a few minutes, to allow everyone to catch up. We stopped for a longer break to have some water and he slumped down in the snow. He was still not wearing his glasses and his eyes had puffed up and blistered around the edges. He had snow blindness. He had lost about eighty per cent of his vision. The enormity of having a partially sighted leading guide was diffused by another drama.

Ella and Amanda had dropped a little behind our main group, but the distance did nothing to soften Ella's frightened crying. Jane, who was walking just behind me, had dropped down into the snow up to her thigh. She pulled her leg out and carried on. When Ella came to the same place, the snow caved away revealing a crevasse in front of her. It terrified her, meaning, to her, that every patch of snow had the potential to fall into a crevasse. She would not cross the gap that had opened up. She stood, hanging on to Amanda, crying and shaking. Karma produced a rope from his rucksack and we were all tied together at intervals of ten paces. Seeing that she had a line of people roped to her on the other side of the crevasse finally forced her across, clinging to the rope and shaking her head to clear her tears.

We had been climbing for five hours and still the pass seemed to be no closer. The laughter and conversation that had filled the early part of the day had gone. We now trudged in a silent line. All of the guides had dropped to the back to try and extract some kind of route plan from Chetram. I was at the front of the rope, climbing through the thick snow. I was still excited by the day, and the idea of getting over the pass made the snow seem easier. I could hear Jane behind me and her breath was forced and uncomfortable. There was a drag on the rope as she stopped.

'I'm not going to go any further.' She sat down in the snow.

'That's a particularly good idea.' I was not in the mood to be sympathetic.

'Shut up.' She stayed in the snow.

Will had caught up with her now.

'Get up and try a bit harder.' I pulled on the rope to try and lever her up.

'For Christ's sake, I've been trying for the last two weeks, while you've been sitting there thinking you are Miss Bloody Perfect.' She jerked against my pull, but she got up.

I started to walk on.

'If you have a moment to come down off your pedestal perhaps you would like to ask the rest of us what we would like to do.' She was walking right up against my back so that I would not miss any of the tirade.

'Sure, what would you like to do?'

'Have you any idea how irritating you can be?' Her sentences were coming with great, sucking breaths.

'Well, I'm sure you are going to tell me.' The personal assault did not really sink in; the pass was more important than that.

'Bitch is not quite the right word, but I'll find it. I've got the whole bloody mountain to find it.' I may have misheard, but there seemed to be a creeping note of humour.

We shouted at each other and I tried to climb faster to get away from the abuse that was pouring into my back, but the altitude put a stop to any show of temper. We had to give up in the end because we were just running out of air, but it left no unpleasant taste, rather a relieved outlet of emotion. Our movements were slow, and we had to stop every few strides to allow our lungs to try and extract some oxygen from the thin air. The day had already been long.

At the tenth false peak the pass came into view, the prayer flags and mound of stones backlit by the sun. The last stretch up to the pass was with the wind in our faces, whipping down from the peaks with icy blasts. It had become an ugly battle to the top.

When we reached it everyone seemed to disappear, hurrying out of the freezing wind into the shelter of the leeward side. Amanda and I laboured up to the prayer flags. We huddled around them with Black hugged to us. I set up my camera on the remote control. The moment my gloves came off my fingers began to go numb. The little control that set off the camera refused to come out of its slot. I wanted to throw the whole thing against the pile of stones and run out of the wind.

'Count to . . .' Amanda shouted at me, but the last word was lost on the wind.

'What?' I screamed back.

'Count to ten.'

I did, and the control came out of its slot, I got my hands back into my gloves, and we took the picture.

'Let's get out of here.' Amanda got up and ran out of the wind.

I stood up on the top for a few moments, leaning against the wind, waiting for a feeling of achievement or delight. We now seemed to be higher than most of the peaks, reaching up into the clouds. But it was the clouds that took away from that moment of exhilaration. They were rolling in a thick, black bank at the same speed as the rapid wind. The sun had gone and the view was disappearing as the snow closed in. We had to get down. I did not look over the side of the pass that we had just come up to see if the porters were on the last stretch up to the prayer flags.

In a few minutes the bleak pass had become a white-out. We were waiting behind a rock, as far out of the wind as we could get, to move off down the other side of the pass. We had been climbing for seven hours and we still had no idea how much longer the day was going to go on.

Cherram could hardly see by now and he was in pain. Sonam was to lead us down.

Through the silence of the heavy snow came a roar. The sound rolled around the peaks and then funnelled up the gully that we were in. It was the sound of an avalanche, but we could not tell whether it was coming from above or below. The roar died but it was immediately followed by another one, longer and louder than the first, but of no determinate direction.

Sonam started away from the rock and I followed behind him. We fell into a close line, controlled by the rope, but now this had become an added difficulty. The snow had a crust on it that felt as if it was going to hold when we first stepped on to it, but then it gave way under our boots, dropping us into the thick, wet snow. It meant that every few strides, one of us was likely to lose our balance and pull the rope line to a halt. Amanda and Ella were at the back and Ella was falling every few strides. Sonam was moving through the snow as fast as he could to try and get us out of the avalanche area. His speed was pulling Ella and Amanda faster than they wanted to go. The loss of visibility meant that it was hard to judge at what speed we were moving. There were times when we stood still, but it felt as if we were continuing forward, as if the ground were moving under us. It was eerie, and came with a shot of motion sickness, as our bodies tried to establish whether they were going backwards or forwards.

Our progress was a series of bursts of speed followed by pile-ups in the snow. Ella and Amanda were getting weaker from falling and the fact that we had not eaten since breakfast. We were into our ninth hour in the snow and we were tied up in a blizzard, losing most of our energy falling and righting ourselves.

'Sonam, can we stop for a moment?' I called to the figure in front of me, his form smudged by the blizzard.

He stopped and the line came in behind him in a ragged fashion. Ella's face was strained from the fear that she had been feeding on throughout the day. We were all wet and tired. I was not sure how much more we could all take. Will and Jane seemed to be finding it easier, but the adrenalin that we had all been climbing on was running low.

'Chocolate mems?' Karma appeared out of the gloom with his hand buried inside his rucksack.

He produced two small bars of chocolate. When he took the wrappers off they were grey underneath, where the buttermilk had sweated through, but they were a shot of sugar. When your energy reserve has been run low even a small amount of glucose gives you a little more mileage, and that chocolate was a temporary panacea. Sonam was told to slow down and we untied ourselves from the rope to give us more freedom of movement. Nobody asked how much further we had to go in case the answer sapped away the small quota of confidence that the chocolate had supplied. It was not until much later that I discovered that we had covered two days' walking in one day because Chetram could not find our proposed camp in the conditions, and Karma was adamant that we should not camp anywhere that could be in the path of an avalanche.

There was a moment during that blizzard, when our sense of direction had disappeared and our muscles were burning, when a page in a trekking guide to Pakistan and India came back to me. It had advised taking as much hard exercise as possible leading up to a Himalayan trek. But it had warned that no amount of exercise, in a controlled environment, could prepare you for the rigours of trekking; climbing day in and day out with your muscles in rebellion and your heart trying to balance the blood flow at high altitude. Nothing we had ever done would have prepared us for that day. Even Will's sweat-ridden stories of gasping up and down mountains with sixty-pound backpacks in the army, began to dwindle after that day.

We were in a gully and we could see neither backwards nor forwards, but just blindly stumbled on down, praying that we would not become glacier fodder. Sonam strode on, a little slower now but still driven by a desire to get down. Four of the porters had caught up with us. Two of them were carrying nothing and the others only had small loads.

The rest of the porters had refused to come over the pass. There seemed to be a mixture of reasons. Oribadur and a couple of the other porters could no longer get enough air into their damaged lungs to walk, so the other men were having to carry them. They had seen the blizzard moving in as our group had reached the pass and they had decided to stop before the last windward climb. The four men who now joined us had been sent on to tell us that the rest would not be coming over the pass. It was hinted that men further up the mountain would turn back and return to Camp One with all the tents and supplies. Karma waved his hand to silence the porters and signalled that we should continue on down the mountain.

The gully began to narrow and rocks appeared through the white blanket. The snow began to thin and peter out. As it turned to slush, we dropped out of the blizzard into the lands of Spiti. Through the trails of cloud we were presented with snow-blasted peaks falling down into a sinewed valley, where the skin had been torn back to show the structure of the muscles in taut reds and browns. At the bottom was a flat floor, dissected by busy tributaries running into the river. The valley sides were lined with rock forms like great, overblown termite hills, standing proud from the muscled rock strata.

We had come into Kipling's 'valley of leagues where the high hills were fashioned of the mere rubble and refuse from the knees of the mountains . . .'. The sun came through and the whole scene was lit up for us. We stared, awed children at their first firework display, rooted where we stood.

We slipped and scrambled over the wet rocks that led down into the valley, willing the sun to stay so that we could sit and recover and look around at this place that we had entered.

When we got to the first level terrace of the valley it was still in the sun. We washed in a stream, screaming in the cold, but laughing with relief that we had made it over the pass, despite Chetram's snow blindness, the blizzard and the avalanches. As we rinsed our socks, Karma was brewing chai and the sun was beginning to drop away down the valley. We felt that we were finally safe, but as the sun sank, all the warmth was sucked out of the valley, and the chai went cold in the cups before we had managed to drink it. Still there was no sign of the porters. We had one tent, one sleeping bag and no food. We sat around the gas stove and watched the side of the mountain, waiting for the porters to appear out of the snow line. No one came.

It could have been that Karma had a touch of the soothsayer about him, or that he had dealt with porter rebellions before, as his rucksack was a bottomless pit of vital supplies that day. Tashi had a two-man tent and a couple of sleeping bags in his rucksack, but Karma produced a tent, a sleeping bag, the gas stove, a kettle, chai supplies, and when it seemed that we would have no food, he found some dried soup in the recesses of the sack. He lent us his sleeping bag, which meant that the guides had only two between the four of them, while we had two as well. We huddled together in the tent, almost too tired to drink the soup that Karma produced, but aware that we needed something. All it did was activate our hunger. We lay together under the two sleeping bags, opened out to cover as much of us as possible, and tried to sleep. Will and Jane found it easy; but for the rest of us, the cold slid up our arms and legs, numbing them and making it harder to find sleep. Will's snoring was not something that we had been faced with before, but as he was pinned on his back by the bodies on either side of him, his long nose became a megaphone, and we huffed and moaned while he growled.

The hours waited without moving as we stared at our watches, longing for it to be light again, so that there would be a chance to be warm and fed. At some point in the round of hours the dogs started howling and scrabbling up and down the stones outside the tents. We looked out into the clear night to see shadows coming down the mountainside. The moon was white enough for them to be able to pick their way down in better visibility than we had during our earlier descent. Within a couple of hours all the porters were down in the camp. Karma ignored them until the morning, but Ella and Amanda left us to find their own tent and sleeping bags. Jane was asleep and the idea of finding our tent seemed too difficult. I had found a patch of warmth against Will's shoulder and I fell asleep as the dawn light began to sidle in.

Waking up was like surfacing after a long illness. We sensed the dry, icy air and the eggshell sky. We could feel our bodies becoming aware of the pay out that they had made the day before. Turning my head towards Will was like forcing an old gate on rusted hinges. His face had a layer of dark lizard skin, blistered around the mouth, with red and puffy eyelids. The tops of his ears were shiny and angry where the skin had swollen, and his lower lip was bee stung. I laughed at the caricature that he had become during the night, but my throat was so dry that no sound came out.

Will said nothing. He did not open his eyes, but lay contemplating the various painful areas of his body. Jane lifted her head and her skin was also stretched and livid. My face felt tight, though no more so than it does sitting in front of a fire after a cold walk, but my nose felt as if it was bristling with needles.

The blast of cold air that came in when Karma opened the tent to bring in the bed tea was like hot water on raw skin. We all recoiled and he laughed at us, but his hand flew up to his mouth as he split his blistered lips and blood bubbled through on to his chin. He peered at us through slits in the middle of his swollen eyes.

We emerged from the tent, a group of explorers, blistered and wincing after just those few days up in the high snow. Above us was the white light of the snow line, below, the valley arched in ochres, reds, browns and yellows. The river jumped around the stones in the bottom. Ella was already out there, squatting on a rock in the river, scrubbing at a pair of socks.

Some of the porters were creeping around the camp, but Karma had made them pitch their tent on the terrace below us in a sort of camp-site Coventry. He rounded us up from where we sat on various rocks, examining our blisters and kneading cramped muscles.

The guides dug deep into the supplies again to give us a breakfast to make up for the lack of food during that long day over the pass. There were omelettes, chapattis, baked beans Indian style, porridge, freshly baked bread and some tired fruit. We were almost at the stage of forgetting how hungry we were and breakfast soothed some of the pain.

We had crossed the pass into Spiti, but the drama of the passage had bred its own anticlimax and we were all listless.

As the makeshift camp began to be packed up, Ella and I crept down to the porters' tent with Disprin, a pot of honey and a kettle of freshly boiled water.

Oribadur was sitting outside the tent, his strained face tilted towards the sun. I squatted down beside him, and was about to touch him, when I realised that he was asleep, his chest rising and falling with shallow breaths. We handed out cups of a mixture of boiling water, honey and disprin; the honey to try and give the sick men a little energy and the Disprin to help with the pain. At Mantalai, when we had made our last full Florence Nightingale round, there had been a queue of porters waiting to cough at us and groan as we felt their breathing. Now there were only three of them who seemed to be genuinely suffering. I was standing over the porter who had deteriorated at the same speed as Oribadur. Beside him was another porter, who had lain at my feet in a crumpled heap at Mantali, claiming that he could not walk, let alone carry a load. Now he was play fighting with another porter, rolling on the floor of the tent, while managing to keep a bidi alight at the same time.

'I'm delighted to see that you have made such a full recovery.'

He asked Jangrabadur what I had said. I doubt Jangrabadur translated my exact words, but the other porter did have the grace to look a bit sheepish before resuming his fight with the bidi still clasped between his lips. When we left the tent, a few minutes later, I heard him spit in my direction. Ella was ahead and out of spitshot, but I turned, my hands together as in prayer, and bowed to him in the formal local greeting. He laughed straight at me and I probably blushed.

When we spoke to the guides in Hindi, or they taught us new expressions and tricks of pronunciation, they seemed to respect us for our attempts at their language. They laughed when we made obvious mistakes, but it was not cruel laughter, rather relaxed amusement that we were finding something so hard that came naturally to them.

Language in India has a class structure of its own. There is no common 'Indian Language'. If you wanted to travel from the tip to the toe of the country, talking to the locals as you went, you would have to be a polyglot with a mastery of fourteen major languages and over 200 local dialects.

The predominant languages are the Dravidian based Tamil in the South, and Hindi as you go North. Once you get into the mountains there is a myriad of Pahari dialects with versions of Tibetan, or Buddhist, as the mountain people sometimes describe it. You may be a fluent Tamil speaker, but you would get further in Delhi with English than Tamil.

English is the language that the British Empire forced on the country as their language for politics, wealth and aspiration. Delhi society flits between Hindi and Oxford-on-Ganges English, as they moan about the government and the state of their country. In the clubs and drawing rooms of refined Simla there is a recurrent theme:

'I am telling you that we would be better off now if the Britishers had not walked out on us.'

These upright characters, in their blazers, cravats, and bristling moustaches, tell you in BBC English, that they regret the passing of the Raj. Their class weapon is clinging to the vestiges of the Empire in the form of the clipped English that they speak. These were the young men and women who cheered Independence at midnight on 14 August 1947, then watched with mounting fear as their country began to cannibalise itself. They looked on as their former maharajahs turned to politics, rousing political rallies to violence and destruction; the same rulers who had once been under the control of the Viceroy. Now, in their dotage, they wish once again to see the firm hand of the Empire policing their streets, running their bureaucracy, and organising an elitist social life which the establishment Indians could join in and feel secure.

The South rebels against the idea of having Hindi as the official language. Communication between the people of the North and South is usually in English. Paddy speaks English with the rise and fall of his native speech pattern, fertilised with vowel sounds honed by English schoolmasters. He sometimes pushes sentences back to front, turning the meaning on its head. The common element is that all his speech, indeed most Indians' English speech, is in the present tense.

'I am telling you Justine . . . *Achchhà*, this thing is very good, very good that we are doing these things.'

I may laugh at some of his expressions when I hear them on a long distance line, but they bring with them a flood of India. To his fellow-countrymen Paddy sounds like an Englishman. In his home town the locals ask him why he does not have a better command of Hindi. His retort is to throw up his hand as an Indian and swear in English, rising up and down the vocal scales like a misplaced Welshman.

[95]

'Bloody hell, this is all rubbish. Hindi is a bloody silly language and I cannot be speaking it.'

It is almost impossible to practice your Hindi in Indian society; they would consider themselves socially inadequate if they did not speak to you in English. The moments when they do break into Hindi are the times to be wary. They use their language in the same way as parents spell out words when they do not want their children to know what they are talking about. There are times when it is useful to keep your knowledge of Hindi to yourself. It can be an effective tool when trying to do business in India.

Even though our language efforts with the porters made me despondent, the guides made up for it. On the easy days, when conversation was part of the journey, we would chant our way up the mountains, counting in Hindi, or practising singsong shop counter conversations.

'*Namaste* ("hello", with the hands clasped together and a small bow),' said the shopper.

'*Namaste*,' said the shopkeeper.

'*Kitne paise?* ("How much is this?")' asked the shopper.

'*Hazar rupees.* ("A thousand rupees"),' said the shopkeeper.

'*Yeh bahut mehnga hai.* ("That is very expensive"),' said the shopper.

And so we would go on, learning useful phrases such as 'How much is your daughter?' (Sonam felt that it was important that we should know this, probably for Will's benefit rather than ours), 'My friend has drowned in the monsoon sewer', and 'Would you like me to sing you some history songs?'

There were times when what they told us we were saying was probably a highly censored version of the truth. No doubt we trilled up and down the scree merrily reciting things more suitable for Raymond's Revue Bar than language lessons, but it made the guides smiling tutors. The one that caused the most amusement was when I asked Karma to teach me how to say 'I am not married because I have not found the right man.' We went through it several times and he laughed more with each reciting. I shall not give his version here in case it risks the wrath of some religious potentate, but it is not a phrase that I shall practice when asked the perennial Indian male question of why I am not married with a large brood. I trust Karma, but I am wary of his sense of humour.

It seemed as if the Indian guides were flattered by our attempts to speak their natural tongue rather than the English that the Empire had forced upon them. Yet the Nepalese porters were insulted, as if we were presum-

The chicken children in Pulga village in the Parvati Valley

Nomadic yak herders on their way down to lower winter pastures

Chetram, the only one of us to have been over the pass, beginning to suffer from snow-blindness on the way up to the pass

Left to right: Jane, the author and vital umbrella, Ella, Amanda and Karma on the way up

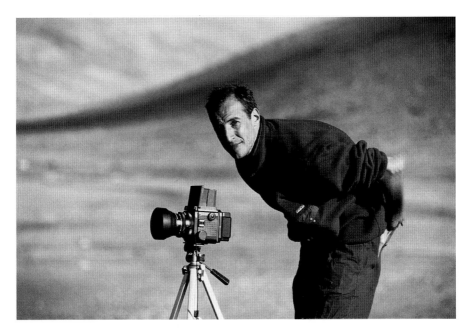

Will, the sole man amongst the gaggle of women going into Spiti

Jane, the author and Chetram, the guide, roped up to get over the pass into Spiti

The road down from Mudh village past the stupa

The man with the glasses and his friend from the blue house in Mudh,
pose statically for Will

A boy from Mudh village bringing in the barley for threshing

The young monk from the rooftop in Mudh who entertained Jane and the author

Off to lunch after morning school. Novices at Tabo Gompa

A performer in the Gompa percussion section

The face of modern Tibet in exile

The lunchtime rush in the kitchen at Tabo Gompa

The kitchen of the blue house in Mudh

Looking up the Spiti Valley from the road at the end of the walk

ing an added authority over them by trying to learn their language. They regarded our feeble efforts with a suspicion that we might use it as a weapon against them.

Ella and I walked away from the porters' tent that morning, feeling less inclined to go back again with Disprin and sympathy. I hoped that we had not offended the guides by appearing to know better than they did about how to treat the porters. I think Karma and the boys were wise enough to recognise the British female passion for clucking over ailing people and animals. They felt that it was all part of the journey. Allowing us to feel humanitarian was another aspect of the service that Paddy would expect of them.

Nobody wanted to rush away from the camp. There were too many wounds to lick. Chetram was sitting on his rucksack by one of the streams washing his feeble sunglasses. They were the kind that you find in crackers. The arms were too short for his ears, they pinched across his nose, and the lenses were just plastic with a coat of dark spray. His eyes were still swollen and blistered, but the short night seemed to have given him a wider field of vision. Someone had a spare pair of glasses and his cracker ones were grabbed away from him. Amanda had some essential oil of camomile, believed by homoeopaths to be a great soother and healer. It was mixed up with some water and Chetram was pinned down with two camomile pads over his painful eyelids. This became quite a sensation and the camomile cure seemed as if it was the latest great invention from Western science. Chetram was proud of his loaned glasses. They were a pair of RayBans, a status symbol in themselves. Once equipped with his new sunglasses and soothed by the camomile, he seemed more enthusiastic about setting off across the scree.

To call it scree is a slight misnomer. Previous experiences had been spent hurtling down steep, smooth slopes, treating the scree like snow, while listening to Will shouting instructions on how to get the best out of a scree run. This earlier variety had been fine and loose, almost like gravel. It had given when I bounced down into it, lifting me when I had jumped out of it. That scree running had been sport and we had gone out of our way to find slopes to scrabble up and bound down. The scree of Spiti was not the same thing.

Scree is made up of rock fragments, some are small and fine, others great lumps of boulders that scatter across the mountains; huge building blocks thrown aside by the giants of the Himalayas. We were faced with the latter variety that morning in Spiti. It was another challenge, jumping from rock to rock, never lifting our eyes from our feet. But we had got through the longest day and we were out of the path of the Pakistan floods. It made the scree seem less exacting.

7

A VIRGIN PLACE

THE explorers and adventurers of the Arctic and Antarctic must yearn for a tree or a plant, anything green growing amidst the endless horizon of lifeless white. I have never been amused by the joke about killing an over-domesticated lap dog by dropping it in a snow field and watching it try to find a tree until it bursts. Poor Black had looked so humiliated as he had spent two days squatting in the snow. The first tree that came through the scree after the pass was sprayed with great enthusiasm.

Even in the arid lunar landscape of this new valley the plants fought through. In the bright sun the sculpted sides were splashed with patches of flowers like the spray from the palette of an excited artist. These were the flowers of autumn, that brief moment before the snows descend into the valley again. As the size of the scree decreased the plants climbed through. There were patches of wild thyme, giving off its scent in the morning sun, bright bursts of purple columbines, red and yellow salvias, and small clumps of wild orchids, their curved petals speckled like a thrush's throat.

Tashi, Jane and I sat down to wait for the rest of our group to catch up and a swallow-tail butterfly landed on one of the fragile orchids beside us. The flower drooped under the weight but the butterfly hung on, fluttering to keep its balance. It seemed strange to find something in exquisite, tiny detail after the great white open spaces, especially a swallow-tail balancing on a mountain orchid. Tashi accidentally stepped on the orchid when he got up, but the butterfly managed to fly away.

The heat of the sun was bright and intense and we began to peel off layers, leaving the carefully wrapped scarves protecting our burnt and blistered faces. For the first time since we had left the lower slopes of the Kulu valley, we were down to shirts. We were dry and warm, our dark, weathered faces a sharp contrast to our pallid limbs. Will and Amanda had taken to shorts and the battle for the tan commenced. I was too vain. Since the fall at Khirganga I had been walking with an ugly brace around my knee. It was thick, flesh-coloured and jointed at the sides. It reminded me of the back pages of Sunday magazines; the ones with pictures of blue-rinsed grannies in nasty arthritic supports. I did not want it on show, neither did I want to have a pale white patch, sandwiched by a mountain tan, on either side of my frail knee.

Perhaps the guides had been premature in their trust of Spiti's fair weather. At the same time, to the minute, as the blizzard had started on the pass the previous day, fine sleet began to come down through the sun. We were soon bundled up in our over-used layers while Amanda and Will's shorts clung to their goose pimples. It was frustrating to be in bad weather again after all the jovial re-assurances that it was never wet in the Spiti valley. But the sun continued through the sleet, the walking was easier, and we were on the right side of the pass.

Jane and I were walking together, deep in conversation. It was a very different mood from our battle up the pass the day before. It already seemed a long time ago. Once we had dug through the usual family problems, we got on to the ticking time bomb of marriage. Jane was still trying to sort out whether she was going to fly back to Australia, into the arms of her rough-edged farmer. London had made her even more confused. The city rush after the big open spaces had been another reason to get back to the 2000 acre paddocks, the sun and the flies. Spiti was her thinking time.

'I'm glad you came.'

'Does that mean you are going to ask me about Australia now?' She was walking beside me, the first time we had been able to do so on the terrain since the early stages of the trek.

'As we are all still alive, you'll probably start thinking about it when your blisters give you a chance.'

'I'm not very sure how I feel about it now. I was so desperate to go back while I was in London because I just really wanted to get away from being back. But now that I am up here I can see very clearly all the things that I would miss about England, and the things that would irritate me about Australia,' she said.

'I just woke up one morning after a couple of years there and knew that it was time to go home. No reason, everything was going well. I just knew that I wasn't going to spend the rest of my life there. So I went out and bought my ticket. But then I never had the love tug holding me there,' I opinioned.

'Well then don't give me any advice if you don't understand the love thing. I'll ask a Spiti yak herd, he'll give me a straight answer.' She crossed in front of me to end the conversation.

We went on to safer ground, but she was still thinking about her dusty love affair while we cooed over other people's blissfully happy marriage start-ups and the drama of new families.

There was no great dilemma consuming me. I had been through mine and it had been no more profound than trying to decide whether to go on, or to head back down the mountains, through the mud. Ella had a mottled life story, Amanda was at the end of a career and Jane was trying to decide whether to wed the Australian Bush dream. Will did not wear his problems on his sleeve; his dramas were no worse than not being able to take great snaps in the rain and his newly discovered allergy to dairy products. Neither Will nor I had come to the mountains to redress any emotional seesaws. We had come to see Spiti with the greed of ambitious travellers, but the others had made us less single-minded in our approach to the delicate infrastructure that we had climbed into. As the area rests on the left shoulder of Tibet, it too is in the cupping bowl of over two thousand years of Buddhism; two millennia of meditation, pacifism, and the Eightfold path that Amanda and Ella were planning to tap.

The West has created its own word for the Buddhism of Tibet, 'Lamaism', to differentiate from the other branches in the tree of the faith that Buddha started teaching after those first nights under the Bodhi tree.

I turned to Amanda for the continuing saga of the Buddha's life.

We stopped for a water break and Amanda walked away with her drawing pad. I followed her and stood beside her when she settled down to draw.

'When Buddha started to teach did he set up schools?'

She looked up and I was prepared for a withering look but she put her pad down.

'He gave his first sermon at Sarnath near Varanasi,' she started.

'I've been there. It is an extraordinary place. Just watching the Hindus going through the ritual of burning their dead on the banks of the Ganges tells you more about the religion than a thousand books.' I had been amazed by this city that is the jewel in the Hindu religion.

'It seemed appropriate that he gave his first sermon there since he was from a background of Hinduism himself. He wasn't creating a new religion, he was trying to find a purity beyond Hinduism that would mean an escape from the painful cycle of rebirth. After that first sermon he gathered a fervent following of disciples. He spent the next forty-four years of his life as a beggar monk, wandering around India, teaching as he went. During the Monsoon his new converts would build halls in his honour so that he and his disciples did not have to sleep in the parks of the towns where they were teaching.'

'A far cry from the dancing girls in the wet weather palace,' I interjected.

Amanda looked at me with an unamused expression and decided to ignore what I had said.

'Buddha saw teaching as the route to Nirvana. In its basic form the ideals of Buddhism are quite straightforward. The problems have arisen from the faith being adopted by so many different cultures; each one tailoring it to suit their national nature.'

'But they must all come from a single source of ideals.' I could sense complications heaving into sight.

'They do and it is quite easy to follow the five main streams of Buddhism that have come from the source.

'Theravada is the oldest school of Buddhism.

'Mahayana is the second school. It is much more liberal in the ways that it interprets the beliefs than the strict constraints of Theravada.

'Zen is the Buddhism of China and Japan. It centres on meditation and is seen as the revolt of the Chinese mind against the intellectual Buddhism of India.

'Vajrayana is the most difficult to nail down. It's all wrapped up in mysticism. The followers believe that they must try and pass from their outer appearance into the emptiness beyond where they can face the absolute.' She looked at me to see if I understood.

'But why isn't Tibetan Buddhism one of the main groups?' I was confused.

'Oh, it is. Lamaism has been around since the seventh century. Before Padma Sambhava brought it in from India the Tibetans followed the Bön religion; a kind of shamanism based on worship of gods and demons with a lot of human sacrifice, devil worship, cannibalism and sex orgies thrown in. Padma Sambhava blended them together. The resulting faith was a bit of a softener on the natural warrior nature of the people of Tibet. He was quite crafty the way he managed to turn the national nature of Tibet on its head.

'He set up monasteries around the country but there was a low point in the eleventh century when the monks became vague with the laws of celibacy and wealth. There was the usual round of decadence, incest and homosexuality. The faith fell into disarray until the fourteenth century when a dual system of leadership was introduced. When monks broke the rules they had to answer to the higher authority. The Dalai Lama came into being as the ruler of the worldly sect. The Panchen Lama, the spiritual leader, came a little later. Both of them are seen as reincarnations of earlier lamas.'

'Why is the Dalai Lama now embraced by all Buddhists?' I asked.

Amanda wrinkled her forehead and thought for a moment.

'I think it's a combination of two things. When the Chinese began to oppress the Tibetans and the Dalai Lama was forced to escape he became a hero for peace. This was underlined when he won the Nobel Peace Prize. He has become the personification of all the calm that is preached by Buddhism and he has been embraced by all the Buddhist sects.' She got up and stretched.

'I find it difficult to understand the lines of reincarnating lamas,' she said as she picked up her things.

'Just wait until we get to the *gompas* (monasteries). Every sharp novice claims to be a lama while we all open our eyes wide and nod our heads. Very few of them are. Not every lama is a monk and certainly every monk is not a lama. If you ask one of the senior monks how many lamas they have at the gompa it usually turns out that there is one or maybe two. That is not to say that two lamas happened to alight at that gompa. It means that the gompa honours two lines of reincarnating lamas. Abbots are appointed by the monastic board to fill in between the generations of lamas. They run the daily life of the gompa until a young lama comes of age.'

Amanda looked at me with amazement as I spoke.

'How do you know all this?' she asked.

'When you have been told by the hundredth nine-year-old novice that he is a lama you start to ask questions.

'Does the reincarnation work in the same way for all lamas, from the Dalai Lama down?' She was walking just behind me, listening to what I was saying.

'Yes, when one lama dies his spirit simply passes into another body.'

'But it seems to be at odds with the idea of Buddhism breaking the cycle of rebirth,' she said.

'They don't see it as rebirth, but rather the passing of a single valuable soul from shell to shell.'

'I remember a story in the papers a little while ago about the baby in

Italy that turned out to be the reincarnation of the lama from one of the main Ladakhi monasteries. They seemed to pin the whole thing on the fact that the baby had a similarly unusual birthmark to the last lama.' She came up beside me.

'The paparazzi usually get hold of the ones that are at all weird or wonderful. Usually the reincarnated lamas are found in the villages that surround the gompa of the late lama; a floating soul can't always be expected to cross the globe. Once the monks hear about a child which is showing signs of rapid development they keep a weather eye on its progress.'

'What is the actual process that a child has to go through to prove that he is a true reincarnation?' Amanda asked.

'Once a rumour has made its way to the gompa gates about a particular child the monks send out a delegation to visit the child and his family. They usually take some of the late lama's favourite possessions with them. They put the potential young lama into a room with his usual toys and the things that they have brought from the gompa. If he starts to play with the lama's possessions the monks have grounds to continue their investigation.'

'But a two or three-year-old child is going to be fascinated by anything a little bit different, whether it belongs to a lama or the old goatherd down the road,' she said.

'It doesn't seem very sophisticated, but when you talk to monks who have been involved in the selection process they enthuse about the children. They describe the sense of calm that these young lamas instil in those around them, the way they speak with the minds of ancient men of learning in languages that they have no reason to understand, let alone speak.'

'I can see why people tend to be cynical about Buddhism. You have to have a tendency to believe in magic.' She smiled and walked on ahead to catch up with Karma.

As she walked away I could hear her beginning to hum something, almost under her breath. I wanted to check with Karma about our next camp-site so I jogged to catch up with Amanda and him.

Karma was humming a circular verse. I tried to make out the words by walking closer behind him to catch them as he sang. It seemed to be the same thing that Amanda had started to sing. I tapped her on the shoulder and asked her what it was.

'*Om Mani Padme Hum.* It's the *Mani* mantra. *Om Mani Padme Hum, Om Mani Padme Hum.*' She chanted it in the same monotone as Karma.

'It's the mantra of Avalokiteshvara (the Bodhisattva of compassion and the patron saint of Tibet)'. She continued to chant.

'What does it mean?'

She chanted on.

'Amanda, do you know what it means?'

'He is the Mind-born Son.'

'Really?' I was not quite sure what I was supposed to say.

'Buddha was the human form of Avalokiteshvara' she continued.

'Is that what you chant when you are meditating?'

'Yes, it is one of the mantras that we use.' This second rash of questioning was beginning to irritate her.

I let her walk on with her mantra and turned to Karma.

'Why do you chant?' I asked him.

'I am reaching the gods. All things in the world have a name and all mantras are made up from these names.' He seemed to be delighted to tell me about it.

'But what are you chanting now?'

'The *Om*. It is three sounds, "A-U-M".' He twisted his mouth to give a clear sound to each letter of the *Om*.

'"A" is Brahma, the cosmic body of the universe; "U" is Vishnu, cosmic mind; "M" is Siva, cosmic knowing. When I say "*Om*" I am saying "I accept".' Karma was comfortable and eloquent with his subject.

'So if "*Om*" means three things, what does the rest of it mean?' I asked.

'It says "Hail to the Jewel of the Lotus", but each piece means different thing: "*Om*", gods; "*Ma*", antigods; "*ni*", humans; "*Pad*", animals; "*me*", hungry ghosts; "*Hum*", hell. You wait, you will hear and see it in all the places we go, all over, everywhere. On stones by the road, carved on wood in children's pockets, chanted in gompas, printed on all the prayer flags.' He stopped for a moment.

'Do you believe all of that?'

'I no understand.' He shrugged and smiled, again reverting to his old cry of not being able to understand me, despite his moment of English clarity.

Karma used the mantra to clear his mind, to calm him and to settle his concentration. For Amanda it seemed to be a form of escape, something that she could dive into when she found that the conversation, or her fellow travellers, did not suit her.

I had reached a wall with Amanda. It seemed as if bricks were coming down with everyone else, but with her it was solid, freshly cemented, electrically wired and topped with broken glass. I could see that it was difficult for her to watch someone else being in charge when she was so used to taking that role, but there seemed to be no regular pattern to her behaviour. When I finally felt that I could predict how she would answer a question she would throw back the antithesis, knocking me off balance by suddenly being on my side. Watching her use her Buddhism was watching her trying to find an escape from her dislike of herself. She portrayed herself in her pictures as the tiny character in the corner, clasping her head and crying out to have a bigger place in the scene. It gave me a little more insight into her soul-searching but it did not make her any easier to understand.

Karma's chanting face was calm and smiling; Amanda's was creased in tight concentration, her forehead forced down over her eyebrows, as she drove her way into the mantra. It was not the time to question her further about Buddhism.

We came to a steep lip where the scree dropped away into a protected gully. This was not a gully like the bleak, windy ones up on the pass. It had a close-cropped covering of grass that seemed to be much brighter than the grass before the Pin Parvati La. It was a smooth, flat area that was a bowling green after the scree. The area was divided by a thin stream bouncing through the grass. Where the ground level dropped down there were miniature waterfalls. It gave us a compartmented camp with three separate areas, divided by the loop of the stream; one for the cook tent, one for the porters, and one for the sleeping tents.

When the camp had been set, I went down to the porters to collect my bag. It was lying in a pile with all the luggage. It was stained by the rain, mud and snow, but amongst the backpacks and hessian sacks, it still managed to look quite smart, as if it had been misplaced at an English county railway station. I picked it up and set off across the green turf to our tent. Black was beside me. We could so easily have been walking across the lawn of a genteel country house to embark on a weekend accessorized by labradors, jolly girls, and boys with loud laughs.

Several things could be attributed to my sense of elation that afternoon: the relief of getting over the pass, the comfort of a landscaped camp-site, or the dramatic valley sides around us, dressed in their Florentine layers. It was a good, tight feeling in my chest, the kind that breeds spontaneous laughter and the strange need to dance and shout. Black and K Nau got the laughter when they presented themselves outside our tent, with sorrowful expressions, their back ends firmly attached. A dip in the icy brook was their salvation.

There was a different audience for the dancing and singing episode.

I had walked away from the camp to try and find a good place to take a picture. I found a rock to stand on that gave a good view. As I climbed on to the rock 'Lara's Theme' from *Dr Zhivago* came up from the recesses of my mind. There was no reason for the trigger. I just saw Julie Christie on the tram and Omar Sharif struggling to catch up with her before his heart gave up, while Maurice Jarré's haunting melody circled in the background, prodding my tear-ducts. The photograph was forgotten and I sang and danced, my camera as my partner, dipping and twirling around the rock. It was still warm from the afternoon sun and the rain had stopped. The camp stretched away in front of me, a velvet green sanctuary. There seemed to be every reason in the world to dance.

The sun was beginning to slide away and, as it cooled, my dancing became more like a dervish, spinning in an ungainly fashion until I was giddy. I stopped and collapsed on the rock as I ran out of breath and lost my balance. I was panting, red-faced and excited. There was some clapping from below the rise that I had been dancing on. I stood up, swaying and unbalanced. Three of the porters were squatting in a row, mid-crap, enjoying the ridiculous cabaret. A sweat of embarrassment broke out along my spine. My dancing had certainly relieved the porters' constipation and my display was simply the camp laxative.

I ran back down and straight into our tent.

Will was skipping up from the cook tent in just his long johns and a sweater, bouncing around under the thin layer of his leggings. Once again his radio was clasped to his ear.

'Over a thousand dead in Pakistan and 125 in Kashmir,' he said.

'That's the same number of people that were at my prep school.'

'Nice thought.' He looked at me quizzically.

'I hope they haven't left too many families behind.'

'No, it was a whole village that was wiped out according to this.' He patted the radio. 'There's some chai down there and I think Chetram is hoping for another eye bath.' He set off up the slope to his tent.

The chai was cold and Jane was picking at her blisters. I joined her. Hers were bigger than any of mine, so I put my socks back on and fussed over Chetram's eyes.

'Where are Amanda and Ella?' I asked.

'They're steaming up their tent with meditation.' She pulled a long strip of white skin off the back of her heel and waved it at me.

'Are you going to eat that?'

'Don't be disgusting.' She examined the piece of skin.

'You would if I wasn't here.'

'Probably.' She looked at it more closely.

Karma was watching us.

'I'd like to have a go at meditation.' I said.

'You can't just do it on a whim.' She threw her cold chai and the flap of skin out through the opening of the tent.

'Who's going to break into the meditation to get the camomile for Chetram's eyes?'

'Will can.' She put her socks back on, tugging them up over her raw blisters. 'Shit, I hate my feet. I'm not going to be able to walk tomorrow.'

'Of course you are. We get to the first village tomorrow and we can find you a witch doctor. Cow dung is supposed to be a very good poultice for everything; I'm sure yak dung will be just as good.' I took a picture of her as she painfully put on her second sock.

'I want to find that piece of skin to show Will.' She peered at the grass outside the tent. I helped her, but Black was skulking away, probably chewing.

She left without putting her shoes on. The sun had just disappeared out of the valley and she was a grey figure walking away from me in the twilight.

Supper was an event that evening. It seemed to have been days since we had all sat together without a mounting sense of panic. The guides had boiled up enough water for us all to have a strip wash. We dug out dry clothes from the bottom of our bags. The only thing that remained lank and dirty was our hair, but that had almost gone full circle and seemed less offensive than when it was first dirty. It seemed far less offensive than it had after the initial week of not being washed. Once again we were able to have the front flaps of the tent open while we ate. A couple of weeks earlier we would have winced at the thin, cold air. Now it was a pleasure to be able to see out into the night without a mist of rain clouding the mountains and the swing of stars above us. They were so bright that when I reached my hand up towards the sky the stars seemed to be at the ends of my fingers.

We came to the first *Mani* wall the next morning. It was like a large table built of pieces of flat stone. Each stone had a few words of a mantra carved onto it. The most common ones were *Om Mani Padme Hum*, lovingly cut into hundreds of pieces of stone; solid prayers piled one on top of the other for generations. Amanda and Ella fell on the stones as if they had found the key to life. Karma immediately slipped into his guise of religious instructor. He translated the mantras to his rapt audience, running his fingers over the carved symbols, caressing the loops and lines

[108]

of the *Om*. Amanda had some wax crayons and they made tracings of the stone mantras, using their wax carefully and slowly like schoolchildren on a first outing to a brass rubbing centre.

Will had decided to view it from a different angle. He was stalking around the stones, crouching down and trying to line up pictures, waving us out of the way when we came into the shot. It was rare that we were allowed in a picture. He wanted to capture a view of a deserted place, where the tourists had not yet marked the landscape with lurid colours and loud, weatherproof fabrics. Jane and I squatted beside the stones, on the opposite side to where he was taking pictures, so that we were out of his line of vision. We were talking and idly picking up the stones around our feet. I was juggling two smooth pieces and, in a cack-handed fashion, dropped one. When I leant down to pick it up again I noticed that it was carved with part of the *Om*.

'Do you think I'll be cursed if I put it in my pocket?' I whispered.

'If you tell Amanda and Ella you will be.' Jane started to turn over stones to see if she could find a fragment as well.

'I've got a piece of the Berlin Wall at home. Someone said that if they gathered all the bits of the wall together that the tourists took away they would be able to rebuild a three mile section.'

Jane ignored what I was saying. She had found another piece and she was looking at it in her hand.

'The Berlin Wall was a bit different because that was being taken down anyway. If every tourist decides they want to take a bit of mantra stone home to fill their house with good vibes, the locals will not be able to carve them fast enough.' I had closed my hand over the piece of stone; halfway through the crime.

'It's a bit that has fallen off. It would just get kicked onto the path and down into the valley by a yak or something. It's not as if we're taking them off the proper pile.'

'We could just put them back with the rest of them.' I had put the stone in my pocket.

Amanda and Ella were reverently folding up their rubbings of the stones and putting them into their daypacks.

'It might be unlucky or against Buddhism or something.' Jane put the stone she was holding in her pocket as well. 'Come on.'

I wanted to put the stone back, but it was too late, and I felt that I was blowing it out of proportion. It may have been a small fragment of stone, but it represented more than that. We had just put pieces in our pockets and walked away.

That piece of stone sits on my desk now. Sometimes it is a comfort and I pick it up just so that I can feel it in my hand. It brings back the colours and views of Spiti. At other times it is a reminder that I broke my rule of travel conduct: took something from a culture that had not been offered, but it had been justifiable because it was "just another little piece of stone".

We were now walking along a path that curled around the side of the valley, following the path of the river. We climbed up over a gentle fold and there was a dark stain against the side of the valley where it curved away from us a few miles further down. As we walked on the stain grew and separated turning into houses and small fields. The houses began to come into focus with windows and doors, the windows outlined in black with green or red frames, the roofs layered with branches and packed earth to act as insulation. They were simple, whitewashed buildings with flat roofs, each one a plain square shape. As we came into reach of the village the static dot that we had first seen came to life.

The small fields on the edge were full of activity, women and children harvesting barley. The women were crouched down in front of the standing barley gathering bundles of the crop in their arms, cutting it with small, crescent sickles. Their plaited, jet hair was tied up in bright scarves. They were dressed in layers; light undertrousers with long tunics, and several faded shawls, tied around their shoulders or belted into their tunics. Their skin was the colour of antique, polished wood; the older women, dark rosewood, the younger ones, walnut, and the children, satin-wood. A few of the women had babies bound tightly onto their backs, their little faces pressed against their mothers' flowered shawls. When they opened their eyes they were as dark brown as the nutty hides of their older relatives. Their mothers wore their dowry jewellery, even while they were out harvesting. In their ears were fine strings of seed pearls, hanging four or five strands together, and caught at the top in a star or flower of turquoise and coral. The weight of the earrings was supported by another strand of pearls pulled up over the top of the ear, to take the strain away from the earlobes. Some of them wore more seed pearls around their necks; others, lumps of turquoise and coral strung together in heavy necklaces.

The great chunks of turquoise are understandable as it is a stone indigenous to these high valleys, but the equal predominance of coral and seed pearls was difficult to fathom in an area so far from any coastline. It was the traders of the past, making their way through from the south of India and China before 1950, who brought the pearls with them. The mountain people exchanged their wealth of turquoise, gold and silver for the marine jewels that the traders carried.

The features of the faces in the fields varied. Some of them had pronounced bone structures with long fine noses, high, arched brows and generous mouths. They would not have been out of place if you put them in an olive grove in southern Italy. In the older women these patrician mountain features became almost caricatured. Their noses resembled beaks, the skin pulled in tight below their sharp cheekbones, their lips fuller and their eyes framed by a web of lines. These were the features of the North Indian blood of Spiti. They were outnumbered by the flatter faces with their sunken, almond Tibetan eyes, ironed noses, rosebud lips and high sloping foreheads. In the children the eyes were little dark raisins that disappeared when their faces creased into smiles, and their lips, kisses that flashed from a pout into a wide smile in a few seconds.

To start with they did not notice us coming towards the fields. They carried on with their work, cutting and laying the barley to dry in careful lines, with the ears pointing down the slope so that any rain would run off them. The field beyond had been harvested earlier and the barley had dried to a pale sand colour. Here they worked in teams of two, one woman squatting down to be loaded by another, until the barley reached right up to the top of her head. Then she was helped up by her loader, counter-balancing the weight by leaning into the slope. The carriers then set off, up towards the village, their faces forced down towards the ground by the weight on their backs; their children hanging onto their tunics, or running in front, while their mothers moved slowly up the hill.

An old woman in the cutting field stood up, straightening out her back from the squat. She saw us and yelled to the others in the field. She covered her face with her hands and cackled with laughter. The others stood up and began running towards us, their bright scarves flying and their faces creased in smiles.

The only real crowd-puller in our midst was Jane with her blonde hair and light eyes. They all wanted to touch her hair, but she was not keen to be mauled. Will had his camera out and the woman who had spotted us first took control.

She had one lazy eye and a hooked nose. Her smile was stretched over her few remaining teeth and her voice was shrill and penetrating. She was not happy for Will to just take random photographs. She herded the children together and stood behind them with her gaping smile. He pretended to shoot a reel of film until the toothless matriarch seemed content with her exposure. He then sat patiently on the ground among the children, explaining to them how his camera worked. To start with they were nervous about looking through the little glass square, but when they saw how it trapped their whole village inside one small box, they became fascinated. Each one wanted to focus on his or her home. When Will zoomed the lens he took them, through the windows of their distant homes, to their familiar surroundings. Some waved when they saw their friends or relatives brought in close by the lens. They seemed surprised when they looked away from the camera not to find the figure right in front of them, but just a dot far away in the village.

Karma wanted to move on from the anthropology scene beside the barley field. He had some bartering to do with the head men of the village to establish somewhere for us to camp. He shooed the children away and set off. The matriarch was not to be fobbed off. She chatted away full of confidence that we understood every word she said. When we moved on again she came along with us leaving her sickle lying beside the last bundle that she had been cutting.

Most of the women and children stayed in the field, unsure of how to behave. A few joined the matriarch. She seemed to have decided that we were her property.

It was the end of the afternoon as we came into the village. The white light of midday had softened to a chestnut gold, throwing tall shadows in front of the yaks that were being brought down from the day pastures further up the valley.

Yaks are a merry sight, like large cows in thick fur coats. Their heavy tails are somewhere between a pony's and an African fly-swat. They have a cumbersome look but they move fast when the mood takes them. They are used for ploughing, threshing, riding, carrying and milking. Even in death they are effective. Their thick coats protect the people through the winter freezes, and their tails fly from the top of prayer flags, dancing in the wind with the mantras.

The men who had been so rare in the fields now began to appear from the shadows of the yaks. Their sons were with them, some of them hanging on to the yaks' tails, or running after those that strayed away.

The bossy matriarch was waving and shouting at them to hurry down to meet the new arrivals. Karma was having an animated conversation with one of the more senior-looking villagers about our camp-site. We were surrounded by a gaggle of children all wanting to see their house through Will's lens. There were people moving around in the village, doors were opening and shutting, with people coming in and out like cuckoo clock characters, and there were dogs, chickens, goats and yaks all over the place. We had arrived in the village of Mudh.

We had become so used to our own company during the previous couple of weeks that this sudden deluge of sound and vision was a metropolitan masala. But Mudh was far from being a metropolis; it hardly made it to the village level.

I have stopped off in one-horse towns in the Australian outback that were groups of just a few dwellings surrounded by dust and tumbleweed. Their fulcrum was the pub; and, on one occasion, the token horse, that had found its way into the bar, was the only one still standing. I have been to ancient tribal villages in the Thar desert in Rajasthan where the Meena tribesmen still kiss the feet of their Thakur (equivalent of an old English squire) whenever he passes by. But in September 1992 Mudh was something different.

In Europe it was Black Wednesday on the stockmarket. In Pakistan hundreds were dying each day in the path of the rain floods. In the isolation of Spiti they were harvesting the barley in the same way as they had for the past thousand years.

This part of Spiti has survived, an anachronism from another era. As the area goes no lower than 10 000 feet, and there is virtually no rain, the shaved valleys are not clothed in vegetation. This makes Spiti the finest rock strata museum in the world. To a geologist it is a taste of heaven.

It was once the seabed that separated the continent of Gondwanaland from mainland Eurasia before the creation of the Himalayas. Part of Gondwanaland was what is now central India. A million years ago Gondwanaland collided with Eurasia throwing up the seabed to create the great range of the Himalayas, the Pamirs and the Karakoram. The rivers and valleys of the Spiti area are a perfectly preserved palette of rock formations from Precambrian to the present day. It is said that the valley has been inhabited for thousands of years, but there is scant knowledge of the area before the tenth century.

Tracing any history in Spiti is not an easy task. As the area has been closed for so long the reference books usually skate over it with a metaphorical wrist wave of history. The few dusty books that did bear fruit agreed that during the seventeenth century Spiti was beholden to Guge, a principality of west Tibet. At that time the people were polyandrous, the practice of women taking several husbands or lovers simultaneously. To mark their importance the women wore the traditional *perags* of Ladakh, the heavy head-dress weighed down with coral and turquoise. Then, as now, their crops were barley, buckwheat and peas. The area prospered as it was an important part of the Hindustan Tibet route and the great caravans of this trading era passed through Spiti. When Guge fell apart in the early 17th century Spiti came under the temporary rule of the Royal family of Leh in Ladakh. It has not prospered since the trade caravans abandoned the high pass route. Now the old paths are only used by local herders, and people like us, determined to find their way into Spiti's Inner Line. The Inner Line is the area that clamped itself shut to all non-nationals when the Chinese invaded Tibet. Even Indians had to get a special permit to get in. The stories of the great art in the gompas of Spiti, and the few pictures of its sweeping canyons and its unvisited valleys, pricked the interest of the outside world. But Spiti kept the outside world away.

The people are not warriors by nature. They have not protected them-selves with battles and long war campaigns. They have practised subter-fuge. There were intermittent attacks from bordering kings over the centuries, but the people of Spiti despatched them with guile. A story is told of one Ladakhi army being fed the local liquor by the seemingly friendly people. Once relaxed, inebriated, and weak, the Ladakhis were massacred by the Spiti people. When the British took over the valley in the nineteenth century they were wary of the local stories and left the region to carry on in the same rhythm as it had for centuries.

The people gave up their system of polyandry to strike a balance between their harsh environment and the survival of the indigenous popu-lation, giving the men a chance to sire more children. Now the eldest son inherits the major part of his father's landholding. The eldest daughter used to get everything, now she just gets her mother's jewels. The rest of the children are expected to become celibate monks and nuns, or live on with an elder brother or sister as unpaid workers in return for their keep. Even now there are still many younger sisters and brothers in families who remain unmarried.

Looking at the group of women around us it was hard to establish which ones were wives and mothers, and which were celibate sisters. The bossy matriarch wore no jewellery that we could see, but she had the authority of one used to wielding the weight of power.

Karma had finished his bartering with the senior men. The site that he had been eyeing as we came into the village had been refused. It was the field where the barley was to be threshed two days later. The day had been selected by Buddhist numerology and the field was being blessed. They did not want it to be polluted with foreign trash. We had been designated a field a little further down, closer to the river.

The porters moved fast, scuttling down the steep slope to pitch camp. Within minutes the tents were up around us and Karma produced chai.

Will headed straight back up to the village, slung with camera equipment, to photograph in the soft afternoon light. Ella followed close behind him. They disappeared into the haze over the barley fields. We could hear the cries of the harvesters as the foreigners arrived in their fields.

The desire for clean hair drove the rest of us down to the river. Our hands were numb before we had even finished rinsing out our socks. Amanda washed in silence, while Jane and I squawked as the glacial water shrunk the skin on our scalps, sending shooting pains through our heads. Jane swore as I tried to rinse the soap out of her hair with fumbling hands. Our hair was still matted and sticky with soap, but the water was too cold to continue. The sun was about to leave the valley and it left us about half an hour to dry before the raw night came in.

We stumbled back to the camp, tripping over every stone with unfeeling feet. Even if we had only managed a stab at washing, the effort had made us feel better.

Amanda had executed her ablutions with far more aplomb. She emerged from behind her rock, her towel tucked around, her hair clean and combed, and with her big boots on the end of her long, skinny legs, to carry her over the same stones that were defeating Jane and me. She stomped effortlessly back to the camp, passing us as we lay in two foul-mouthed heaps.

The twilight brought Ella and Will back from their baptism into village life. They were bursting with tales of the exquisite idyll that they had been exploring.

The bossy matriarch had pounced on them as they set foot in the first field above the camp. Will had been embarking on a photography session, entranced by the children's complete lack of self-consciousness. They just gazed straight into the camera, waiting for something to happen when he pressed the shutter. Their unblinking expressions had sent him into photographic ecstasy. It is so rare for a photographer to find a subject who can stare straight into the camera with an unguarded expression. We have all become so conditioned to adopting our familiar pet pose when a camera appears, that it is hard to imagine what it would feel like to look into a lens with total innocence.

Will was kneeling in homage to his child models, unable to hit the shutter fast enough, when the bossy matriarch's nose swooped into his camera frame. She already had Ella in her thrall. Now she was on Will's trail.

They were led away from the barley fields and the wide eyed children and taken to the village. The matriarch took them to her house where she and her family brewed up butter tea for visiting monks, traders, and now this new breed of arrivals, the first of the tourists.

Her house was on the edge of the village, commanding a central view up and down the valley. No outsider could get in or out of the village without being in view of the house. It was blue while the rest of the houses in the village were white. Most of them had shutters, but the blue house had proper window frames, some with glass in them.

Ella and Will were led into the house past an antiquated figure, perched almost motionless, outside the front door. She was ageless, her nose hooked and her skin gnarled. Her hair was grey and thin but still pulled back in a thin plait that hung down below her waist. Her small body was padded out with layers of clothing that culminated in a yak skin fixed to her narrow shoulders. Her boots were made of leather with toes that curled up at the end. She seemed to be part of the structure of the house until they had passed in through the door. She let out a piercing cry to announce their arrival. She was the door-bell.

They went from the bright afternoon into unlit gloom that smelt of old flesh. They climbed over a pile of semi-dry yak skin before bumping into the first step of the staircase. The narrow climb came out onto a landing with four doors. Only one of them was open and it led into the main room of the house, a miniature kingdom within itself.

Ella and Will's first impressions gave the rest of us an idea, but their descriptions were excited and jumbled. It was difficult to really create a picture that prepared us for what we found when we climbed the stairs the following day.

[8]

BESIDE THE TURQUOISE RIVER

T HE young monk was probably the same age as me, perhaps twenty-four or twenty-five, but it was difficult to be exact. He was sitting on the roof in the morning sun. The light picked up the fine stubble on his head, where it was growing out from the last shave. His face was smooth and his eyes closed. Jane and I had climbed up to the roof. There was a staircase on the outside of the monk's house and an old woman in the alley had made no move or sound to signal that we should not climb up. She had just stopped and watched as we began to go up.

The young monk also seemed unmoved by our appearance. He did not open his eyes for the first few minutes but continued to meditate. He smiled before he opened them so that he greeted us with a serene expression.

'Welcome to my village.' He had a proprietorial tone as he swept his hand across the spread of the village.

'Do you come from Mudh Gompa?' I asked.

'There is no gompa here. I have come back for a week to see my family to help with the harvest.' He got up and stretched.

'So you are on a holiday from your gompa?'

'Yes, I come back for a week two times a year.' He replied.

'Twice a year.' I corrected him without realising.

'Yes, two times.' He laughed.

'You speak very good English.' Jane stepped in.

'Thank you, they teach it at the gompa,' he said.

'Do you have to come far to get back here?' I asked.

'No, it takes about three days. Two days on the bus. A day of walking at the end. I was lucky this time. It was not too hot. There was another monk. So we were twice.' He laughed again.

'How long have you been at the gompa?' Jane asked.

'For twenty years. I will one day have a degree of *Geshe*. (Our closest equivalent would be a Doctor of Divinity. Monks with this degree are well advanced in ecclesiastical law and highly revered. The literal translation is a spiritual preceptor.) I am now well advanced at the gompa and I teach the novices. I am a *gelong*.' He flicked the corner of his robe in an authoritative manner.

'How does a novice get into a monastery?' I asked.

'A boy is sponsored by a friend or relative. The sponsor arranges for teaching and residence at the gompa. Most of the boys are coming in at seven years. If a man has more than one son he is expected to let one train as a monk. Every monk has to have permission from their parents.' He got up and stretched.

'Why do they have to get permission?' I asked.

'The Lord Buddha's father, King Suddhodana, made it a rule that every monk had to get permission because both his sons and his grandson went into meditative orders without his consent.'

'How many stages have you been through at the gompa,' I asked.

'I start as *rapjung* when I was seven. At seventeen I took thirty-six vows and was a *getsul*. I changed from wearing rust to ochre robes. At twenty-one I had to start obeying 250 rules of monastery life. At this time I became a *gelong*, as I am now,' he concluded.

'Do you have other brothers and sisters?' Jane asked.

'We are three. Number one brother is a lama at a gompa near here. Number two has the land because number one is a lama. So I am number three and a monk.

'When I come back my mother takes me to all the houses in the village to see all of the families. We go and sit on their roofs and drink butter tea. It is the taste of my village that we make to keep out the mountain cold. The tea cannot fight the bad taste and it is bitter. At the gompa we drink tea with cardamom and sugar and it is sweet. When I come home I drink butter tea for my mother. It makes her happy.' For the first time he stopped smiling.

'Does your mother live in this house?' I said.

'She lived here from when she married my father, when she was fourteen about.'

'Has your father always lived here?' Jane sat down.

'My father is dead since three years. My mother does not carry the barley from when he dies and her head hurts all the time. So I come back to help my brother who has the land.'

'I am sorry,' I said, as conditioned.

'Do not feel sad. You did not know him.' He was smiling again.

'I bring my mother aspirin from the gompa to help her head. While I am here she can take them and her head does not hurt for a while. This makes her smile again. Do you have any aspirin?' He asked us.

'We have some, but not very much. A lot of the porters are ill so we have been giving it to them.' I felt embarrassed that I was making excuses.

'Aspirin does not help tuberculosis.' His face clouded again.

'How do you know they have TB?' I asked.

'I hear them when they come up to the village to get arak. The cough is loud and porters make the same cough. They kill their lungs, but the arak makes them forget for a while.'

'We will try and bring some aspirin for your mother?' I back-peddled.

'Come.' He motioned us to climb down into the house.

Jane and I looked at each other, unsure of what to do. He started away down the stairs.

'Come, come, we will have some sweet chai.'

'He's a monk, he's hardly going to attack us.' Jane set off behind him.

Sexuality had not entered my mind. I did not feel that we had the right to just jump into the villagers' lives. But this was an invitation and the young monk had taken our silence as an acceptance.

The interior of the house was simple and furnished only with the basics afforded by Spiti life. The young monk's room was in sharp contrast to the rest of the house. It was clinical in its tidiness and there was hardly an inch of space that was not filled with the vibrant accessories of his religious life.

He nodded affectionately at the photograph of the Dalai Lama above his bed and we both made the appropriate reverential sounds. It was a faded picture of the bespectacled leader, who was gazing out at us with the kindly, myopic expression of a mole. The monk waved his hand around and disappeared next door to make chai. For a moment we stood in the middle of the room, unsure whether to stand or sit down on his bed. The latter seemed a little forward for a first meeting with a man of Buddha, so we wandered around examining his collection.

The shelf above his bed was a shrine to the Dalai Lama, with the photograph in the centre, trimmed with bright, patterned ribbon. Next to this was a picture of another man in the same pose and dress as the Dalai Lama. The face was not familiar and the picture was framed with just a simple blue ribbon. On either side of the pictures there were small bronzes of Buddha, smiling with his eyes shut, in the lotus position. These were flanked by incense burners, each holding several sticks. Only one of them was alight, releasing a thin trail of smoke that dissipated into the room. Beside these things, and with equally important billing, was a Boots thermos flask, bathing in the smoke of the incense, like a trophy next to the shrine to the Lamas.

'Perhaps it is a thermos flask that the Dalai Lama drank from.' Jane reached up to take it and withdrew her hand.

We could hear the young monk next door and we did not want to be caught meddling with a relic.

Along the edge of the shelf were a series of little Chinese bowls, the blue variety that you get those side sauces in at Chinese restaurants. They were filled with water and there were unlit candles floating on them. One was alight, with a few petals floating around the candle. It was below the picture of the Dalai Lama.

There was an alcove at the head of the monk's bed. This was filled with small prayer wheels, prayer bells, brass *dorjes* (the Buddhist thunderbolt symbol), and three butter lamps, one brass, one copper and one silver one, each a low, flattened bowl filled with yak butter. One of them was alight in keeping with the belief that a butter lamp should always be burning at an altar or shrine. There were several rosaries, each one with 108 beads, one of which was larger than the rest. They are for reciting the name of Buddha a hundred times, with a few spare for mistakes. The larger bead is to mark the culmination of the cycle. Two of them were made from bone, one was wooden, and the fourth was amber, rich gold in colour with veins of pale honey.

In the corner of the alcove was a large brass jar containing a proud flourish of peacock tail feathers. Their brilliant blues and greens were reflected in rich silk Tibetan wall hangings that hung across the windows. They had scenes of Nirvana with smiling characters floating across delicate bridges in fragrant gardens with a backdrop of mountains rising out of the black silk. On either side of the window hangings were Tibetan *tangkas*, the religious scroll paintings of Buddhism, usually depicting lamas and deities surrounded by scenes from their lives. Once again they were depicted in lustrous colours to convey the wealth of their existence. These colours are ground down from plants and minerals in formulas that are handed down from teacher to pupil in mystical secrecy.

On the monk's bed was a Tibetan prayer rug, bordered with the familiar geometric patterns that we associate with Tibetan loom carpets. These were the same patterns that were around some of the other photographs in the room. They all seemed to be of Buddhist leaders. Any one of them could have been the young monk's lama brother, but it was hard to find a family resemblance.

The one part of the room's fabric that did not fit with the picture that we were building of the monk's life was the pillow on his bed. It had a pretty white case with a delicate frilled edge. In the middle of the pillow was a gold medal. It was positioned in a direct line with the main prayer wheel in the alcove and the picture of the Dalai Lama and his blue ribbon framed neighbour. The importance of its positioning must have meant that it was valuable to the young man; a prize that he laid out on its pretty pillow.

Half of one wall of the room was filled with carefully rolled mantras in their dark red boxes, stacked up like a miniature shoe shop, right to the ceiling. Any spaces on the wall that were not filled with photographs of lamas, or pieces of mantra, were patched with small painted sections of wall hangings, or the A4-sized prayer carpets, woven as miniatures of the larger prayer rugs.

Beside the bed were books in three different languages. A book on Buddhist Phenomenology in Tibetan, a French translation of *My Land and My People* by the fourteenth and present Dalai Lama, and a dog-eared copy of *Frenchman's Creek* by Daphne Du Maurier.

The room gave the mixed impression of an over-crowded Victorian drawing room and an American Shaker patchwork quilt, busy with highly illustrated scenes.

We had probably only been in the room for about ten minutes. It seemed much longer. Each time we were about to nose amongst his possessions we were stopped by the sounds of his tea making from next door. There were so many tidy little corners that gave away secrets about him, but we would not be able to question him as it would prove our probing.

Jane sat down on the corner of his bed.

'Where's your camera?'

'Here.' I pulled it out of my bag.

'Will you take a picture of me? I may never be in a Buddhist monk's bedroom again.' She straightened her back and readjusted her gingham sun hat while I fumbled with my camera.

It flashed not just once, but in a series of lightning explosions, having decided for itself that an orgy of bright light was the best way to capture Jane. We both blushed as the room illuminated like a temporary nightclub.

The monk appeared at the door with a tray of elegant teacups and saucers. They were white, with a pattern of small blue flowers. They were the same kind that my housemistress had given us tea in while dispensing career advice. I know hers came straight out of the Peter Jones china department.

'Good camera, that flash will make better picture.' He set the tray down and started to pour the tea into the dainty cups. Neither Jane nor I spoke.

'What kind of camera?' he asked.

'It's an Olympus. I am sorry. I hope you are not offended that I have taken a picture in your room.' I was formal with embarrassment.

'No, no.' He waved a jug of milk around before adding a little to each of the three cups.

He then put sugar in each, stirring methodically, listening to the jangle of the spoon against the china. It was a smooth rhythm. He smiled, enjoying the sound that he was making.

'I have a camera.' He left the three cups of tea and went over to a small metal trunk in the corner. He opened it and took out a Canon Sureshot. 'When I visit other monasteries I take pictures. It is very useful.' He replaced it carefully in the trunk, locked it and returned to the tea.

'Sweet tea, good to taste, with cardamom.' He handed us each a cup.

We perched on the edge of his bed and he stood opposite us, watching us drink.

'Good chai?' he asked.

'Yes it's delicious thank you very much.' It was not as good as Karma's chai but the novelty of drinking out of maiden aunt china in Mudh gave it an edge on normal tea.

'Does your brother come back and visit?' I asked.

'A week two times a year.' He looked down into his teacup.

'Do you ever come back at the same time?' I had not picked up the slight note of recalcitrance.

'He comes back before the harvest. Lamas do not work in the fields. Monks can work but not lamas.' He finished his cup and turned to the tray presenting me with his back.

I had touched a nerve so I retreated from the line of questioning.

'How long will you be in my village?' he asked.

'Just a couple of days,' Jane answered.

'Good.' From his tone it was difficult to distinguish as to whether he was pleased we were staying or relieved that it was only two days.

'Your mother must be very proud of you for being in such an important monastery.' We had seen some pictures of the monastery on the wall and it looked big enough to be important.

He turned back from the tray, smiling again.

'We are not people who are proud, but she is happy.' He offered us more tea.

He told us a little about his life in the monastery and the novices that he looked after. He sat cross-legged on his bed and described getting the youngest boys up at dawn for the morning *puja* (prayer ritual), and how they all washed at one pump in the courtyard. As he spoke he turned one of the prayer wheels slowly. There was a small ball on the end of a fine chain that gave the momentum to turn the wheel.

The prayer wheel is another verse in the song of Tibet. Most Tibetans carry one, spinning the wheel and releasing the prayers into the air in the same way as the prayer flags flutter their words into the wind. Each prayer wheel, or *mani-chuskor*, is a cylinder holding a long scroll with *Om Mani Padme Hum* written over and over. In the great prayer wheels of big gompas the mantra is written out up to a million times. The small one that the young monk was spinning released his mantras quietly while he spoke to us about his life at the gompa.

The time came to leave. He followed us back up onto the roof and returned to the same position that he had been in when we found him.

'Who was the other lama in the picture beside the Dalai Lama?' I remembered to ask.

'Our last Panchen Lama, the one who leads our spirits. His name means "Great Scholar". Our fifth Dalai Lama appointed his teacher Panchen Lama. From then it is the older of the two lamas who is the teacher to the younger one.' He held his hands out in front of him, offering the information to us.

'What does Dalai Lama mean?' I asked.

'Ocean of Wisdom.' He clasped his outstretched hands together.

We promised to bring him any spare aspirins and he waved as we left. When we got to the bottom of the staircase we looked up. He was sitting on the edge of the roof, staring out over the fields.

'Amazing that he had that camera.' Jane turned away down the street.

'They live a very different life if they go into a monastery. Even when he comes home, he brings that other world back to his room in his village.' I followed her.

'Those cups were hysterical. Where did he find them?' She stopped.

'Peter Jones china department of course.'

'Listen.' She put her arm out to stop me.

There was a loud English voice, straight out of a herbaceous border, coming from a roof just above us.

'Who are they?' it boomed.

We looked up and above us was a plain, florid face, framed by a sensible flowered cotton scarf, knotted tightly under a frumpy sun hat. There was a general babble of conversation and several more faces appeared above us, none quite as severe as the first, but all variations on a theme.

'Come on.' Jane set off towards the entrance of the house that the faces peered from.

We climbed up onto the roof through the middle of the house. Two young boys were playing in some barley that was drying on an internal balcony below where the English voices were coming from. They jumped at us when we appeared, laughing and dancing around us, but apparently oblivious to the crowd scene above. We indicated to the boys that we would be back down again to show them our cameras and admire their antics in the barley. They let us climb on up to the roof.

The English party were huddled together at one end of the roof, concentrating on the view, but more importantly, trying very hard to ignore us.

There was one man with a polite face who did not look quite as affronted as the rest of them. We had a short, slightly terse conversation in ridiculous stage whispers.

It transpired that they were a group from a company who had sold a heavily over-priced package-tour with the premise that these people would be the first foreign visitors into Spiti since time immemorial. They had come into the valley from an area that was not restricted. They had been charabanced to a town called Kaza where they had been met by forty porters and fifteen pack ponies. There were fourteen of them and their pack pony, porter ratio made us feel almost spartan in comparison. When they had signed their large cheques they had not expected to bump into other white faces, especially white faces that had come into Mudh through an area that had not even been considered possible to reach.

Jane and I settled on the edge of the roof to watch the uncomfortable progress of the party. They held their position at the opposite end, talking loudly and keeping their backs to us. In the end our nonchalance drove them away in a cloud of expensive climbing clothes and indignation. The herbaceous border in the headscarf had broken out into a sweat. She huffed at us as she lurched inelegantly at the ladder down from the roof. She stopped for a moment, about to say something. Her mouth opened and closed like a fish, but she said nothing. She huffed again and climbed down.

We laughed when they had gone, probably just loud enough for them to hear. It was a petty rivalry that had broken out in a matter of minutes.

Just when we thought we were high enough in the mountains, and pure enough in our thoughts not to be concerned by small-mindedness, it leapt out at us with a red face and a flowery scarf.

We could see down into our camp and the others had not come back for lunch yet. We stayed on the roof, watching the figures in the fields bent over their scythes, and the English group making their painful progress back across the river. It took them a long time to cross the rope bridge. There were several first refusals, and by the time they had all got across, the line was widely strung across the far bank. Now, from our position on the roof, we could see where they were camped, tucked away around a corner on the other side of the river. It would have been discreet if it had not been about the same size as the Field of The Cloth of God. The tents were the same orange that you associate with train-spotters' anoraks; the variety that always have squashed sandwiches in cling-film in the pockets.

'Do you think they'll sue their travel company?' Jane got up.

'It will depend how they couched the promise that their customers were going to be the first into the valley. Travel agents have the same secret code as estate agents. When a travel agent says that you will be the first to experience the exquisite beauty of the Spiti Valley for seventy years it's a load of balls. They really mean that you will be one of the first thousand.' I could see Will's gangly figure making its way back to the camp.

We climbed down the ladder to find the two boys waiting patiently for us in the barley. One of them was sitting in a conical carrying basket, begging to be photographed. We showed them our cameras and let them slide the lenses, making them laugh as they zoomed each other's faces in and out of focus. They stood proudly for us, their chests stuck out, their hands resting on the upturned conical basket. They were like a Victorian couple posing side by side, but coyly separated by a suitable piece of furniture. The difference was that these two were dishevelled, their faces dusted with barley chaff rather than rose powder and their toothy grins wide and unselfconscious. When we left the house they followed us down the street, dancing around us and jumping in front of the camera whenever they had the chance. They were crestfallen when we tried to photograph anything that did not include them as the focal point.

Will had not been heading back to the camp; he had been making his way to the blue house. We had been told that they were having an afternoon *puja* to bless the incoming harvest. This brought us all to the blue house at about the same time and this was when I got my first impression of the bossy matriarch's realm.

We came into a room lit with shafts of daylight from the windows and there was dust dancing in the angled rays. The smells were as instantaneous as the visual impact. The overriding impression was of drying yak skins mixed with the smell of people living in close proximity with one another. Then came the smell of *tsampa*, the simple mix of ground, roasted barley and water. The top note was incense that came from the corner of the room, by the window.

A travelling monk was busy around a temporary shrine. He had a proud face with dark skin and stretched Tibetan features, as if his eyes had been pulled up towards the top of his ears. He was setting up a farmyard scene of small animals and people, moulded from barley flour, butter and honey. The tiny group was terraced on several levels up to an image of Buddha. He sat at the top, serene in the Lotus position, his benign expression unfocused and smiling.

A teenage girl was sitting close to the monk, her legs spread under her thick tunic and apron to catch the bits of dough that were falling off the figure that she was fashioning for the monk's collection. Her face was an almost perfect sphere, untroubled by bone structure or facial plains. She was bent in concentration over the tiny *thorma* (ritual harvest) figure that she was making, stopping only to flick away her plait when it dropped over her shoulder and to raise her head when we came in.

The transient monk was preparing for the harvest *puja*. The little figures moulded from rough dough were the Spiti equivalent of the Christian Harvest Festival baskets; the apples, plaited loaves and tinned fruit that spill over the altar steps each September.

The blue house was to be the scene for prayers to bless the threshing field and give thanks for the crops that had been gathered in. But there was none of the parish pomp that makes small children fidget in their pews. It was just one monk who had taken over the corner of a busy kitchen.

Next to the girl moulding the figures was another aged figure who could have been a book-end with the door-bell woman outside the house. This character seemed to have a little more authority, perhaps granted to her by her hub position in the kitchen, rather than being outside the front door. She was rocking backwards and forwards over a cabbage, crooning to herself as she slowly shredded the leaves into her lap, flicking them from her apron into a large bowl. Most of the cabbage landed on the floor but a younger relation was on hand to gather granny's leaves into the bowl.

Behind the granny there was a doorway into another room. It was small and most of it was filled with a large drying frame. A window at the side sent a shaft of light across the frame making the thin strips of drying meat glow dark red in the sunlight. The meat hung in twisted shapes, contorting as it dried in the layers of the frame, like a macabre mobile. Squeezed in beside this was a long shelf that dipped in the middle where it carried the weight of large cans of dried milk, small vats of oil, and several large jars of coffee, as well as preserved vegetables that would have looked more comfortable in a laboratory than a larder.

The room moved from a centre-piece, a fireplace set in a pot-bellied stove with a smoke pipe that made its rather haphazard way out to the roof through the ceiling. The protagonists in this kitchen drama were gathered around the fire involved in various aspects of cooking. One girl was squatting on her haunches making *tsampa*. She was talking to another character who could have been a cousin or a sister. This second girl was pummelling the butter tea, pounding the ingredients together in a long wooden churn. Two other younger girls, who were probably no more than seven or eight, were scrubbing at root vegetables on the other side of the fire, their bodies crouched over bowls of dirty water. One of them was bent so low that her plaits had trailed in the water. Choreographing this whole performance was the bossy matriarch. She was not actually doing anything herself except running a very effective campaign of delegation.

In that one room was a concentration of activity, both religious and domestic, each one fitting around the other in a comfortable fashion, working in homespun harmony.

We were greeted with great enthusiasm, particularly by two men crouched a little way from the central action by the cooking fire.

These men had dark, weather-beaten faces and one of them wore a rather smart pair of glasses. They were dressed in a mixture of layers, thick with months of ingrained dirt. They wore traditional, heavy woollen trousers that had adopted the colours of the landscape. The one with the glasses had a mat of shaggy hair tied back in a beautiful sky blue ribbon. He wore a woolly hat on his head, the kind worn and loved by Benny on *Crossroads*. His shirt had lapels that could have taken flight. Over them was a plaid jersey, the variety that you usually see propped against the bar in The Ferret and Firkin. Both of the men wore the same kind of shawls as the women, pulled tight around their shoulders and fastened with a motley collection of safety pins. I would have liked to have asked the man with the glasses where he had found his 1970s catalogue clothes. They seemed so out of place amongst the traditional mountain weaves; but after a closer look around there seemed to be a lot of catalogue garb. It was

[127]

unlikely that one of those telephone directory-sized catalogue companies had found its way into the Spiti Valley, but we seemed to be surrounded by living proof. To make up for the bad lapels and nasty jerseys, both men had rows of heavy earrings; large lumps of turquoise and coral hanging from small loops in a line that dragged down their lobes.

They both jumped up from where they had been squatting and herded us towards a long, low table in front of the window. On the other side was an even lower bench that you could only sit on with crossed legs. There was some frantic arm waving and we managed to convey to the matriarch that we would like to have a look around before she pinned us down on the low bench. The two men returned to their places, following us around the room with their eyes, as we inspected the various corners of action.

We admired the *thorma* figures that the girl was making for the *puja*. We watched the monk as he laid out the last of the characters in the rural scenes. It may have been something to do with our arrival, but he seemed to think that it was important to put on a very dirty, red windcheater that was neatly folded beside him. He zipped it right up to his chin and then pulled a separate hood out of the pocket. He put on the hood, pulling it tight under his chin with the drawstring. He did not seem happy about this new look, so he undid the string and carefully rolled the sides up. He had now made it look like a child's paper boat, floating on his shaved head. This pleased him. He gave us a satisfied smile, drew himself up with a deep breath, and resumed his arranging tasks.

The only way to hide the laughter caused by this millinery exercise was to cross the room at speed to explore the larder. Even just turning back into the room, and catching the spectacle of the monk's boat hat, set it off again. The moment was diluted by the arrival of Amanda and Ella. They appeared in the door, blinking from the dark staircase.

The matriarch soon had us all lined up with our legs crossed on the bench under the window. We were served tea in pretty china cups by the girl who had been pounding the urn in front of the fire. This time it was not as easy to swallow as the young monk's cardamom scented version that Jane and I had enjoyed before.

Yak butter tea, or *gugur* tea as the locals call it, is a curious invention. It was created for a purely practical reason, which is something that you have to bear in mind as you swallow it. Its taste comes somewhere between the sensation after a bad dunking in the sea and trying to drink the lumps in curdled milk. It is an acquired taste. The ingredients are green tea, salt and butter, topped up with boiled milk or water. They are pounded together in a long wooden churn, like the one in the kitchen of the blue house. The wooden casings are usually engraved with delicate carvings; scenes from the fields with yaks and herders, clouds in the sky and even tiny birds. The churns are just as much family heirlooms as the dowry jewellery around the women's necks.

The ingredients each serve their own purpose. The salt is to compensate for the amount of sweat that is lost at dry, high altitude. The butter is to give fast energy in an easy form to insulate the drinker against the rigours of the climate. The tea and milk do their best to fight the foul effect of the salt and butter, but it is a losing battle. If you are in a kindly household you are advised to drink the tea down quickly while it is still hot. Once it starts to cool the butter coagulates and the gelatinous lumps are not only nauseating to swallow but can be very effective in giving you severe and immediate diarrhoea. The best way to behave in the face of butter tea is to think of international relations and knock it back fast.

We were trapped, cross-legged, with butter tea in front of us and no escape. The two men had been joined by three young boys. They were hunched in a row with their arms folded across their knees waiting for the tea to go down. The first cup was an ordeal and there was a moment when it came rushing back up again. We managed to escape a second helping by setting up a photographic shoot that wholly absorbed everyone's attention.

I have a crafty gadget on my camera that allows you to take photographs with a remote control button, rather than sprinting back on a self-timer and hanging on the edge of the picture looking foolish.

We set the scene with the window as the centre-piece. The five of us were lined up on the bench with the monk beaming on our right, proud with his sailing boat on top of his head. The foreground of the shot was crowded with whoever could get their face in front of the camera. Several of the pictures came out with just one blurred face, making a bid for stardom as the remote control was pressed. The two men sat with fixed expressions and the same eagle stares that had followed us around the room earlier. It was a pose that we were to see again with the same characters, but fixed in a different setting later on. Behind them the monk's shrine stood out in vibrant relief from the slinky puce pink piece of satin that it was arranged on, the pinkness giving all the butter lamps and cymbals a rich glow. Above the monk's head was a shelf with two large tins of powdered milk. Both tins had ugly teddy bears on them, their colour matching the negligee pink of the shrine cloth. Next to these were two old pots. The first was highly polished silver with delicate engravings and three stubby legs. The second was darkened clay with pretty, faded paintings around it. They were the tea and sugar pots, the central vessels of the household.

Above the shelf was a bad photograph of a family group comprising the man with the glasses, the matriarch, the cabbage-bashing granny, the two young girls and a small boy in the robes of a gompa novice. They were all smiling into the camera with slightly anxious expressions; the matriarch and the glasses man with proud hands resting on the shoulders of the novice. This indicated that the former two were husband and wife, though they gave scant evidence in their behaviour. He seemed to be a kitchen accessory that she found mildly annoying. He tended to ingore her shouts and orders. It was just your average marriage.

Will's tripod was set up at the other end of the room with my camera screwed into the top. He was in charge of the action button as he had the longest arms and the remote control baulked at long distances. Each picture shows him sitting next to me with the little black remote control in his hands. We have big open expressions, except for Jane, who is not showing a double row of fixed teeth. She has a slightly more guarded look. The monk's face does not change from one photograph to another, except for one picture in the middle of the series where he is taking a curious sidelong glance at me.

I remember the moment very clearly.

'Right, are we all ready?' Will waved the little black button over his head to indicate that the photography was about to begin.

Everyone nodded or agreed verbally. A few of the younger ones clung outside the picture and the granny and her cabbage had no intention of coming anywhere near the whole circus. She remained unmoved, occasionally waving her savage knife at us in a vicious but unfocused fashion.

Will took the first picture and we all stared at the red warning light, waiting to be immortalised. The flash was the same as it had been in the young monk's bedroom, creating temporary lightning in the room. All the locals jumped or laughed in surprise, not knowing whether to duck or run out of the room. Once we had established that it was harmless we continued. The first picture has a room of dazed faces except for the five photograph-hardened tourists. After that a few more of the peripheral characters pushed into the picture. The red light was flickering, just before the flash.

'Say "money, money, money",' I shouted out.

Everyone laughed, even if they did not understand, except for the monk.

He looked at me out of the corners of his eyes. I caught his sidelong glance and it was full of confusion. He knew what I had said, but it did not make him smile.

The remote control button gave up and the photography was abandoned. The afternoon *puja* was about to begin.

I had expected a great silence to descend on the room, followed by a shuffling as everyone came to sit around the pink shrine. The two men and one of the boys resettled themselves by the fire, facing towards the shrine. Everywhere else in the room life carried on undisturbed. The granny resumed the cabbage attack with renewed vigour and the younger girls went back to their tasks, cleaning vegetables and making *tsampa*, their fingers covered in the sticky grey mixture of ground barley and water. The matriarch had put another apron on over the one that she was already wearing. As the *puja* started, she took up the main position by the fire, almost pushing her husband over to get there.

Will leant over to whisper in my ear.

'I've been to these before. We will be here for the rest of the afternoon if we stick the whole thing out.'

'Will there be a natural break at any point?' I was conscious of the monk watching us.

'Not really, but the whole thing is fairly casual.' The monk crashed his cymbals above Will's whisper and it began.

The *thorma* figures were scattered with barley, a couple of them toppling over in the grain downpour. The monk began to chant mantras as he threw the barley, the granny chopped on, the butter tea continued to be pounded in the urn and the matriarch blew her nose loudly on her sleeve.

For the first half hour we sat in rigid silence, hardly breathing or moving. The monk continued with his mantras, punctuating them with loud throat clearing, then gobbing into an old dried milk tin beside him. At unheralded moments he would hit a small hanging gong, or chime the cymbals, or, on a couple of momentous occasions, he chanted, gonged and clanged all at the same time.

During one of these loud interludes, when we were heading for the first hour mark, I leant across to Will again.

'Is it just going to carry on like this?' I asked.

'Yes.' He had his eyes closed and he did not even bother to whisper.

I had a look at the others. Amanda still seemed to be deeply involved, but Ella's concentration had begun to flicker. Jane was sitting on the end of the bench sticking the end of her shoe laces in and out of the threading eyes. The monk gobbed and got up. He stretched and walked around to

the back of the shrine to rummage in his bag. I looked at Will and we
got up at the same time. The others followed suit without any encouragement. No one else in the room either took any notice or cared. We left
in embarrassed silence.

It was mid-afternoon by the time we got back to the camp. Karma was
pacing the cook tent with a plate of cold chapattis. We told him that we
had been to the *puja* and he signalled that we should sit down to eat. He
had that exasperated expression worn by women when men disappear in
different directions whenever food arrives on the table.

We dispersed again into the village after a late lunch. Jane, Will and I
headed off together.

Most of the fields were empty now except for one near our camp. The
two men from the blue house were hunched together in the same position
as they had held in the kitchen. This time they had scythes in their hands,
although they seemed to be doing more talking than cutting. They stopped
when they heard us. Will took a picture before they turned around, their
two heads close together in conversation above their static scythes. They
jumped up as we approached. Will waved his camera at them to ask if he
could take some pictures. The man with the glasses nodded stiffly and
stood up straight, having pushed his glasses back up his nose. The second
man stepped further away from his friend and stood in the same ramrod
position.

Will waved his hands around to try and relax them, indicating that he
just wanted them to carry on what they had been doing before, but they
would not move. He jumped around imploring them to just be as they
were. They were posing and nothing was going to move them. He finally
took a series of pictures of their stern faces and fixed stares, as they stood
like badly dressed army recruits in the middle of a barley field.

At the time he was disappointed that he had not been able to capture
the two men in a conversation piece. What he did take was some pictures
of two men standing as sentinels in a field, rigid in the presence of aliens,
ill-prepared protectors of their fragile culture. Their stares were the same
ones that we had seen earlier in the blue house, fixed expressions of
mistrust and fascination.

As soon as we left them they squatted down in the barley again, but
when Will spun round to try and catch them off guard, they were bolt
upright again as bookends in the barley.

There was an upper section of the village where a handful of buildings
clung to a steep sinew of the valley. This was where we were going and
the dogs came too. The lower and upper sections of the village were

divided by a fast running tributary of the Spiti river. There was just a single beam crossing the water and it was dark and glossy with the spray from the fast water.

'Just look at the other side and walk across.' Will strode down to the edge of the bank.

K Nau and Black were ahead of him and Black ran straight onto the beam, scrambled, lost his legs and flopped into the freezing water. Will stopped for a moment and took a closer look before testing it gingerly with one foot. We were close behind, urging him to step out. His boot slid on the wood but he kept his balance long enough to cross. K Nau crawled with her belly touching the beam. Jane and I held our breath and tried to look at the other side. She slipped in and I stayed smug and dry.

The houses of the upper village were silent, the doorways and windows empty of characters. There had been a rumour that there was a collection of nuns who lived in this part of the village. No one seemed to be sure where they had heard the rumour, but we were all sure that it had come from somewhere. One of the bigger houses was the most obvious place to start the nun hunt. It had a narrow outside stairway cut out of the mountain rock. Brave, stunted trees grew from between cracks in the stone where they had managed to find a finger of light to grow towards. The steps did not lead onto a roof, but into a narrow passageway that divided one house from another. Half way along the house it divided into two, one branch leading up towards the roof of another house, the other curving away around the side of the next building.

Will and Jane took the path around the house and I climbed on up. The steps became steeper and narrower, until there was no longer any sign that they had been carved. They had become a series of steep rocks in the mountainside.

Once I was up the silence prevailed. I could see the tiny figures in the village below, moving around the fields and straining under their loads of barley. Some of the figures were standing up, shouting to their friends and family, or calling out to dogs and errant yaks. Yet none of the noise carried up to the rooftop; it was just a bustling scene with the volume turned down. Standing on that rooftop was the first time that I realised the doll's house proportions of the village. Everything seemed to have been built or constructed in miniature version. The houses were small and square with rooms that were not an inch larger than they needed to be. The windows, frames and lintels were half-opened eyes wearing heavy mascara. The animals had tiny proportions, giving the impression of being young. Even the people made my five foot five and a half inches seem Amazonian.

Now that I was so high, the diminutive sizes were exaggerated by the distance and by the vast swoop of the surrounding valley, pouring its enormity into the village. It made the little cluster of homes seem so irrelevant, and yet there were the busy little characters, scratching their mark on the valley sides, refusing to be ignored by the giant natural tracts of land around them.

I closed my eyes.

'There you are.' A voice came out of the silence.

'Ahhoww,' I shrieked as if I had been attacked.

'Woaw,' Jane coaxed, as if I was a horse.

'You surprised me.' I tried to get my breath back.

'It is easy to think that you are the only person in the world up here.'

'Where's Will?' I asked.

'Taking pictures.'

There seemed little point in continuing the conversation. The silence did not ask to be broken.

We took the route down that Jane had come up, squeezing ourselves through the narrow gaps between the houses. When we found Will he was deep in concentration, his eye latched to the lens. A cat was sitting on the branch of a tree above his head, its tail swinging backwards and forwards in languid rhythm. Cats are rare in the high reaches and its presence seemed to indicate something. As with so many dramatic messengers, the cat was black.

'Chai,' came a shrill cry.

We all spun around.

She was tiny, perhaps about four foot ten. Her sex was not the most obvious thing about her. There was the same fine stubble on her head as the young monk, and her ochre robe hung on her thin frame, giving no landscape to her body that was either male or female. After her cry she lifted her arm to run her hand over her scalp and we could see one of her empty breasts hanging like a tangerine in a sock. We had been found by a nun.

'Chai, chai,' she screeched again.

We stood in a line, shaking our heads, the idea of more butter tea bringing us to an instant and unanimous decision. She flapped across the roof towards us and we turned and fled. The dogs had been silent until this point, but they followed our fast escape down the steps, howling and barking like retreating banshees. We stood at the bottom in a pathetic little group of over-excited dogs and embarrassed tourists. The nun had disappeared and the silence returned to the narrow alleyways and steep steps of Upper Mudh.

The sounds of the lower village were comforting after the silent houses and the clanking nun. They were bringing in the last crops of the day, the girls bent double under their loads, moving slowly up the hill to the village. Some donkeys were being driven up from the valley pastures, for the threshing the next day, and the yaks were coming down from the high pastures.

Jane and Will went back down to the camp. I took the upper road and walked back through the village. I was squatting in the shadows of a house, photographing the line of women coming up from the fields; tortoises bent under their loads.

'Hello.' A sweet voice came from behind me.

I stood up, hitting my head on a window lintel above me.

'Shit.' I dropped my camera.

The girl laughed, putting her hand over her mouth, her eyes disappearing among laughter lines.

'I'm sorry.' My head hurt and I sat down where I had been squatting.

She came forward as if to come and sit next to me, but stopped.

'Are you well?' she asked in the same sweet voice.

'Not at the moment, but this is just a phase.' My head was throbbing.

She put her head on one side, unsure of what I had said. There was a pause and then she settled down in the dust beside me.

'My name is Neri.'

'I am Justine.'

'Do you think I am pretty?' she asked.

She was dressed in the same way as the other women but her tunic was cleaner. Instead of a dirty shawl she had a silk scarf around her neck. The only letdown in her outfit was a terrible old pair of shoes. It probably would have been easier for her to walk barefoot than in those ancient, twisted shoes. Her hair was thick and glossy, without the dusting of barley chaff that seemed to cover most of the other women's heads. Her skin was smooth and almost unmarked, apart from the spread of laughter lines around her eyes. She had intense liquid brown eyes and a slightly sad expression behind her smile.

She took her shoes off as she sat down, putting them neatly to one side.

I did not know what to say. I just stared at her with a rather stupid expression on my face.

[135]

'Do you think that they will think I am pretty in America?' The brown eyes were serious.

'Well yes. I am sure they would.'

It is difficult to know what is the right thing to say to a young mountain girl with pretty eyes and lumps of turquoise in her ears. An American might have missed those things and seen only the stubby teeth and flattened, hard-working hands.

'If I find American husband I can have big house with servants and TV for mother and father.' She clutched her knees and smiled.

'You speak very good English. Who taught you?' The same question I always seemed to ask.

'My brother is a monk. He was going to America to learn at university. He telling me all about blue jeans, carports, videos.' She was animated and excited.

'Why do you want to marry an American?' I asked.

'I will not have to work in the fields. I have house and servants and learn to drive car.'

'Only very rich people have servants in America, or people like the President,' I tried to explain.

'My grandfather is not very rich but he has houseboy and he lives in just small village.' She looked at me as if I had said something very stupid. 'I will go to America when I get a new pair of shoes.'

This was the dilemma: I wanted to find a way of telling her about how America gobbled up the naive, but here she was, a pretty girl stuck in a village on the side of a mountain. In her eyes, all that lay between her and a lifetime of winnowing was a new pair of shoes as a passport to the green, green grass of the USA. She had only to look at the deep lines around her mother's eyes, and at her father's back, hunched from years of carrying, to believe that America would give her more than Mudh.

'I don't think you would like the food in America,' I tried.

'You think so? My brother says they are all rich and fat. They eat when they want and they are happy.' She was twisting her hands together in a hungry fashion.

'Rich people are certainly not always happy,' I said.

'Yes they are.' She put her hand over her mouth and laughed again.

I did not know how to argue with that; so, we both laughed and I told her a bit about England. She was intrigued by the idea that my parents allowed me to go out to work and earn money. She wanted to know about bank accounts and how people took money out of the wall in the way her

[136]

brother had seen in America. She kept returning to the question of how much it would cost her to get to America. I tried to translate an air fare into her terms, but she would not believe that people could pay so much money to fly through the air in such a dangerous way.

'I am frightened to fly or go on boat, but I will get away.' She was serious again.

'Once you left Mudh you would realise that the rest of the world is not as good as you might think. You live in a very beautiful place.' I hoped that my idealism did not sound patronising.

'It is not a good place.' She looked down into her hands with her sad brown eyes. I left her sitting in the late afternoon sun, twisting her hands in her lap. I went back to the camp feeling bemused.

Karma was trying to shoo away a group of children who had set up camp around the cook tent. Most of them were little girls with their baby brothers and sisters tied in bundles on their backs in the same way as their mothers carried them. They were a band of miniature surrogate mothers; small girls who stepped in and took over the care of the smallest baby, humping them around on their backs as if they were just another part of their bodies.

'*Tashi deleg.* ("Hello").' This was the extent of my Tibetan.

They collapsed in a pile of giggles and waited for my next faltering attempt. Sonam had a bowl of water that he had been washing cabbage in. He slung the water at the children and they retreated, screaming behind the tent to tend to their bundles who had got the brunt of the dirty water as they all fled.

I wanted Karma to try and find out about Neri. I knew he would be going up to the village with some of the porters to get some arak, so I asked if he could sniff about and find out anything that he could.

Neri was the first character in the valley who had expressed a desire to get out of what we perceived to be a peaceful idyll. She seemed to personify the need of the younger mountain people to seek the greener grasses beyond their valley. We could not sit as a self-appointed authority and tell them that green grass did not grow down in the drought-bound plains. Neri would not have heard if I had told her that all the main railway stations of the Indian cities were crowded with people like her. Their vision of bright lights, big city had been transformed into a beggar's existence on a small patch of ground outside a station. We could not be educators, only observers, and it left us with a sense of impotence and a small understanding of the frustrations of parenthood. Nobody wants to crush the dreams of a sweet girl with a pretty smile.

Karma came back from the village later in the afternoon. He seemed to have extracted some information from the bossy matriarch. Her ability to be a fount of information on every subject, from Neri's life to the smuggling of arak, led Karma to wonder where her grasp of reality slipped into elaboration or straightforward lies. He was wary of the authenticity of her tale, but this is what she had told him.

Neri was the second daughter of one of the major landholders in the village. Her elder sister had nearly died at birth when her mother had gone into labour on the hillside with only her baby son to help. As a result of a difficult birth this daughter had a paralysis on one side of her face. Being the inheritor of her mother's dowry jewels, a marriage was arranged with a cousin from another village. The young bridegroom had been keen to see his bride-to-be before the wedding, although it was strictly forbidden. He skulked into the village, pretending to be a transient herder, and saw Neri and his fiancée in the fields. He went back to his village and told his father that he would only marry his intended bride if Neri was part of the deal. She was eleven at the time.

As the cousin was from a larger landholding than Neri, her family was desperate to make the marriage. Only Neri's second brother, the monk with the broader outlook resulting from a partial American education, stood against the idea. He took Neri away to stay in one of the tithe dwellings of his gompa without telling his parents.

For several months the young girl was looked after by the monks. She was even allowed to join some of the classes with the novices. She proved to have an iron will and an aptitude for languages.

Meanwhile, back at the family fort in Mudh, they had found out about Neri. The still unmarried cousin was sent to fetch her. Neri's brother resisted vehemently until he was told to disentagle himself and the monastery from the affair. The senior monks did not want the gompa to become involved in the family's nuptial scandal. Neri was released to the cousin. He raped her repeatedly on the way back to Mudh. She was just twelve.

Neri's physical condition when she got back was testament to her treatment. The cousin was beaten by her father and the double marriage was off. Both girls continued to live with the family and there seemed little chance that the elder girl would find another match. Neri was tolerated but regarded as trouble, especially as she had continued to educate herself after her return from the gompa. She also started to daydream about America and spend more time on her appearance.

Karma doubted every word of the story. I believed it except for the bossy matriarch's claim that Neri had no memory of being repeatedly raped. A total loss of memory and her burning desire to escape from Mudh did not go together.

I am not sure whether I had decided to fly the flag of feminism or to try and play God, but I went back up to the village to try and find her. I was not even sure what I would do if I found her. Initially I was driven by anger that all the things Karma had told me could happen to one girl and, secondly, I had been roused by his ambivalence. As I climbed up the path towards the blue house I began to formulate a *Boy's Own* plan to release Neri from the shackles of her reactionary situation. I would free her by giving her enough money to get to Simla. Once she was there I could give her a letter of introduction to a friend who ran a school who might be able to find her teaching work. It seemed so simple and heroic on the path through the empty barley fields.

I did not know which house Neri and her family lived in, so I returned to the spot where I had met her. I skirted the blue house to avoid an inquisition and butter tea. Once again the sun was beginning to dip out of the valley and the twilight freeze was beginning to set in. My ardour as I left the camp had sent me out on my mission ill-equipped in just a tee-shirt and unattractive military jungle shorts. I roamed the streets around the spot where I had met Neri but could not find her, or anyone else. I climbed back up onto the roof where Jane and I had found the young monk, but it was empty. I sat for a while where we had seen him, serene in his meditation. I hoped that, perhaps, if I tried to absorb some of his aura, Neri might appear below me on the street.

I was behaving like the puffed up director of a bad, big-budget film, thinking I was omnipotent, yet probably driven by all the wrong ideals. Neri did not appear and I began to get very cold. I could hear someone below me in the street. It was the old woman who had watched Jane and me climbing up onto the roof earlier in the day. I called out to her and she stopped. She looked up and I signalled to her to wait until I had come down.

I scrambled down, tripping on the last step because I was cold and uncoordinated. She did not look so small and old when I was at her feet in a heap, looking up her nose. I did not expect her to speak English so I greeted her in Hindi.

'*Namaste Mataji.*' I mumbled in greeting; it being a mark of respect in India to address someone older than you as mother or father with the reverential suffix '*ji*'.

She looked at me with her hands on her hips.

'How do you do.' There was even a note of sarcasm beneath the thick accent.

'You speak English?' I asked, with surprise.

'Some.'

'How did you learn?' I asked, once again.

'My grandson gives me little knowledge.'

'Is he a monk?' I was getting closer to Neri.

'Yes.'

'So you are Neri's grandmother,' I said.

'Yes.'

The conversation continued with her monosyllabic answers to my prob-ing questions. Her use of English was charming. Her 'close blood dos' were her family affairs and her 'river to the sea', her old age.

She would not tell me where Neri was, so I tried her on the tack of her own life. She sat down on a doorstep, and the twilight from behind the house turned the ridges and puckers of her skin to crumpled suede.

She pointed to the bridge at the bottom of the village and told me that she had only crossed it three times in her life; once when she had arrived to marry her husband and then the return journey to the village of her birth when her mother died.

'I do not cross the bridge more. The barley that my people cut is my barley. The barley I carry, my barley. If I go over the bridge it is just to cut the barley of others, not mine.

'My young people are better here. They cut our barley, not barley of other people. There is no barley in the cities.

'The old goatwoman's husband went to Delhi to sell some things. He is lost and does not come back. He goes.' She held up her hands twice to indicate twenty years. 'I think he is very lost.' She laughed loudly, the sound rattling in her throat. 'The goatwoman is not so sad. He is a lazy man.' She cackled some more and then stopped.

She took my hand and pushed her face close to mine.

'Neri is here with me. She will not go while I am here for her.' She let go of my hand and patted my shoulder.

'Do you have any aspirins?' she asked. 'My head is bad.'

'What is it with you people and aspirins?'

She laughed and held out her hand, right under my face. I had some in my pocket that I had brought in case I found the young monk. I gave her some of them and they disappeared into the folds of her clothes. She patted my shoulder again and walked away.

'Tell Neri that I came back to find her,' I called after her. The money that I had brought to give Neri was burning a hole in my pocket.

She waved her hand over her shoulder but did not turn around.

I have tidied up her speech a little to make it easier to read. She had a habit of turning the meaning of her sentences back to front, and it was all in the present tense, regardless of whether it was past, present or future. It took some time to work out most of what she was saying, but her meaning was easier to understand than her language.

That night the porters got drunk on arak. They sounded like football hooligans. The village lay in silence above us while they filled the night with wild shouting and curdled singing.

THE SONG OF THE YAK

W HEN location scouts are sent out by film directors to find a place that does not really exist they try their best. They run up big bills crossing the world attempting to find the villages that time forgot. It all usually ends with the budget of the film doubling, and a set having to be built from scratch, creating another back-lot façade of a place too perfect to be found. With luck Spiti may be protected from movie stardom by its inaccessibility, but it is unlikely. Perhaps in a strange, roundabout fashion, the slow glide of Buddhism into Hollywood might help defend the untouched pockets of Tibet.

Winnowing day was enough to make any director salivate.

We left Mudh later in the morning than we had meant to because of the after-effects of the arak binge in the porters' tent. While they packed up the camp with more deliberation than usual we took advantage of a sleepy bunch of children who had come to see if we were going to leave any rich pickings behind. Our cameras came out in a simultaneous quintet but Jane and Will were crouched down in front of the children first.

They were a group of ten, the youngest probably only a few weeks old, bound tightly to his elder sister's back. She might have been only as old as eight but she seemed to be the senior member of the group. They ranged in height from knee-high to chest height. Their clothes would once have been an array of bright, rainbow colours, but now they had all been grubbied down to an earthy hue. There were six boys, the baby, two girls, and a small child who was of indeterminate sex. The older boys wore variations of the filthy rolled woollen hats that we had seen dotted around the male members of the village. The senior girl was dressed as a small mother, her matted hair pulled back under a scarf, firmly knotted under her chin à la ER II. She had several layers of tunics on and the baby was bound to her back under a shawl. She was a bossy matriarch in the making.

They stood motionless in a tight unit while Jane and Will's cameras zoomed in and out of their faces. Only the smaller children were not gazing straight into the lenses. K Nau was asleep in the dust beside them in the throes of a hunting dream, yelping and twitching in her sleep. The young ones were intrigued by this dog that talked in her sleep.

I stood behind them and took another in my series of us taking pictures of them. The foreground was filled with a large portion of 'builder's bottom', as Will's walking trousers had succumbed to his loss of weight and slipped down. In front of us were ten dirty faces, some of them cross-eyed from trying to stare into all the lenses that were being fired at them. We caught them on film and waved goodbye. They remained rooted in their photographic poses until we produced a parting shot; a packet of biscuits that we had managed to prise away from Karma. They fell on them until the senior girl grabbed the packet and began a serious division of the booty. It was weighed heavily in her favour.

As we walked away down the river path there was a mist hanging on the valley sides. It seemed to pour down the streets, washing through the people emerging from the village to set up the threshing field. They did not really seem to be walking or running, but floating on the mist. We waved and a few of them waved back, but we were leaving, and they had the most important day of their harvest to attend to.

At the end of the village was a large *stupa* (Buddhist burial and prayer mound). There was a small group waiting to wave us off. They were perched around the *stupa* waiting for the tourists to leave town. We had nothing left to give them, except a few sweets and these were not allowed. The World Health Organisation had made their point. So we kept our sweets. They did not wait around for long when they realised that we were an empty cupboard. I looked back as we dropped down the path and they had all gone, except for one child who was trying to hold onto Black's tail. An older girl soon came and dragged her away. The *stupa* was left white and deserted in the early sun.

Stupas are the furniture of the Buddhist landscapes from Ladakh to Kandy. They are the burial mounds of important religious figures. Instead of adopting the sad Western funereal shape of a prone body, these memorials are domed and spired, reaching up towards the sky. In a deserted landscape, where there is no sign of man nor beast, a row of *stupas* will stand out in their whiteness against the browns and duns of the horizon.

They grow from a simple terraced layer of polygonal bases to a curvaceous dome that rises into a tiered spire.

When a lama or abbot dies they are cremated on the *stupa* sites, sitting upright in a huge urn. It is around this cremation urn that the dome of the *stupa* is shaped. Sometimes the paint is worn away by the weather and the sand coloured *stupas* stand like proud ghosts in the landscape, lined up as if marking a pathway that leads out beyond the horizon.

Our route from Mudh carved a path along the steep valley side above the river. There were sheer drops where walls of winter ice remained unthawed. We slithered and swore our way down, trying to keep our boots out of the icy river and failing. But Spiti remained true to its arid promise and the sky above us was clear.

The valley sides climbed away from the river.

Some divine creator had dived into a large bucket of arak, drunk his fill, and then taken to the valley sides with a chisel. Then he had coated his vandalism with feathered layers of chocolate, planting the teeth of giants at intervals like random candles in his great valley.

Chetram had responded to the tender camomile treatment and his eyes were healing. Once again he was leading us, but it was the last day that he was to be our guide as we were about to reach our destination. He took us away from the river and over undulating sinews of ground that led down to the valley bottom. By now we were on a path that was recognisable. It was just a narrow dusty track, but to us it might as well have been a motorway. To the people of Spiti it was their main road between Mudh and Sangma.

As the day went on the path widened to become a track. We were able to achieve the luxury of walking, talking and looking around at the same time. Because of this we were hardly aware of the approach of Sangma. It appeared over one of the undulations; a location scout's medieval countryside dream.

The track became walled and the idyll opened out in front of us.

Under a haze of flying barley chaff was a crowd of men, women, children, ponies, yaks, mules and donkeys. The animals were tied in lines; the children driving them around the threshing posts; the women and girls forking the barley high into the air. The men were spread around; some crouched, smoking and watching; others driving the animals or coming in from the fields, their conical baskets loaded with dry barley.

The threshing and winnowing scene was alive with noise, the shouting of children and the laughter and conversation of the adults. But the sound that blanketed the air was the anguished cry of a jack donkey in hard pursuit of a disinterested, flirty jenny. It was this call that marked the rhythm of the song of the winnowing yak. The Tibetans have a song, a child's nursery rhyme, based on a conversation between a yak and a donkey. It is a sweet, simple song. I used it as a framework for the yak's song that I found in the rhythms of the valley to create another version.

'I am the yak that presses against the mule that is tight against the pony who crushes the donkey against the threshing post. Round and round we go, the barley under our hooves. The dust rises up into our throats and nostrils, hanging there until all the barley has gone. The sun burns through our backs and pulls the fluid out of our spines. Still we go round with a stick at our rumps in the hands of a red-faced child, screaming as we go on going round. The girls crouch in the fields, cutting, cutting with their blades of the sickle moon. Their barley lands at our feet while we go round, until the donkey calls to me:

'Slow down, fat yak, I am splitting my gut on this threshing post.'

'But I cannot stop because the stick boy is on my rump. We walk on and the grain pops out of its ears. The girls take the yield from under our feet as they sing of their dowry jewels and the river. The chaff flies from their forks, finding our eyes and throats. Then I lift my tail, but a boy is at my rump with a bucket. There is no splash against my hock and the barley stays clean. The boys, the stick and the bucket are always behind us.

'The turquoise in their ears is the same colour as the river, the pearls are the bleached barley beneath our hooves. Their coral is the colour of the eyes of their men when the arak bottle is empty and the night is black. We wait outside in the darkness and try to blow the dust from our lungs. The children come out to feed us before they go to bed. They talk to us and bury their small hands in my thick coat, twisting their tiny fingers among the mats. When I put down my head to eat the donkey calls to me:

'Hey fat yak, move over. I may be small but I have to eat too.'

'Then it is quiet except for the groan as the red-eyed men roll onto the women in the dark to make more sons to drive us around the threshing post.

'In the spring my horns will be painted again and the tassels will hang down and brush in my eyes as I walk.

'The invaders stopped the tassels from being hung on our horns, but not up this high. They did not climb to our place. They say they stopped the painting because they were frightened of the bright tassles of Buddha.

'Our life is good until we become the curled boot on their foot or the stripped hide on their back. We can wallow and drink in the turquoise river when they take us down there at dawn and dusk. Then they lead us up to the high pasture and I can kick the donkey as we climb without there being a stick at my rump. The donkey squawks at me:

'Hey fat yak, try that again and I will bite your tail and never let go.'

'I know he will not bite. He would not dare. He knows that donkeys' tail never flies with the mantras on top of a prayer flag.

'In the summer I wear a saddle and I am caparisoned in bright colours. I lead the way up to the summer pastures. The men ride in front on their quick-stepping ponies, scuttling through the rocks. We move more slowly, swinging from side to side, as we cross the landscape. Some of the women ride on our wooden saddles, clinging to the rope that bites through the ring in our nostrils.

'When we cross the high places the snow leopards find us, sniffing us out in the thin, black night air. Sometimes there are two of them. They break into our rest and fill the darkness with noise. They slide out of the rocks, smelling our warm breath. We feel them and bellow into the night, sensing their jaws in the silence. We run, blind in our fear. The men call out to us in the gentle voices of fathers, but we still run, bumping into each other. Each time I lose my balance I think they have found my throat. Then it is silent again and we can stop and breathe. Sometimes they get one of us, sometimes they fail. They come close enough so that I can see their blunt tails and smell cat.

'Our people dig deep pits and leave flesh in them to catch the cats. They cover them with branches. The leopards smell the meat and drop into the pits. We call with delight when they have caught one. Their coats will buy much for our people. The pits make us feel safe.

'They carry our dung back from the pastures and dry it on the sides of their houses in the sun. The grass that we have cudded is what they burn at night to fill their cold homes with the smell of our rumination. Nothing is wasted here. They burn our muck and the birds pick the barley grain from theirs.

'No part of us is wasted. Our flesh sits in the bottom of the leopard traps, our skin is scraped clean and they wear us to keep warm; we carry them; they milk us; we all give birth in the same fields but our young walk sooner than theirs. They carry their babes on their backs as they sow the barley to grow again so that we can tread it again, around and around. By the time their young walk ours have trampled two harvests. The boy still clinging to his mother's back will probably be the one who drives my young around the threshing post. Then one day, my tail may fly from a prayer flag and my young and their young will see it there. Then the donkey will look up and say:

'Hey fat yak, you really made it.'

The song of the yak is unsung but its words are all around you when you see the yaks in the fields, trampling around the threshing post, in the bundles of drying hides, tied to the top of a prayer flag or in the wide eyes of a new born calf. That moment when they are propped on their spindly front legs, their hind legs curled up underneath them, their floppy ears still plastered against their head with afterbirth. That is where the rhythm of the song of the yak springs from; the same rhythm that drives the animals around the threshing post.

The valley sides rose up all around this animated scene in layers of whipped cream and chocolate, throwing the threshing field into frantic, minuscule proportions. The villagers lifted their hands to wave as we came close, but they did not leave their work. The porters put down their loads by the sides of the field, crouching down among the village men to talk, or just lying back in the sun as the chaff flew over their heads. Will followed the animal threshing lines with his lens, his frames filled with the haze coming from the winnowing and the dust rising from below the animals as they trod the barley.

Jane, Amanda and Ella spread themselves around the field in search of an angle for their pictures. Amanda then moved a little further up the slope to take out her pad and begin to draw the way she saw the scene. I walked up to the edge of the village to find a place where I could look out over the whole scene and try and find a way to describe it that would not, yet again, be punctuated with a stream of 'Me' and 'I'.

Three little girls with their sibling bundles came to stand beside me. I reached out to touch the knotted hair of one of the bundles. The girl carrying the baby pulled away, laughing and ducking from my hand. I left my hand in the air as I would with an animal that I did not want to scare away. The girls stopped a few paces from me and stood looking at my hand. The one that I had reached out to, stretched her hand towards me and plucked at my sleeve. Her wrists were fine and her hands slim and fragile, unlike the spread fingers of the older women. She looked up at me for a moment before hiding her face behind the arm of her baby bundle in a cloud of giggling and crinkled eyes.

These little girls already looked like women; their ears pierced with big loops of coral and turquoise; their faces marked with fine lines from the sun; teeth stubby and misshapen; hair tied back in scarves; in the same way as their mothers and aunts. I sat and waited for them to come and sit with me. Two of them walked away; shouting and laughing at the third girl, who stayed. She was the one who had reached out to touch me. She came and sat down beside me. She looked across and noticed how my hands were resting in my lap and she did the same with hers, carefully laying them one on top of the other. The baby on her back was silent. It did not cry out for attention or demand to be played with. It knew it would get no response, so it lay still on her back. She stuck her legs out in front and they only came halfway down the length of mine. She was so small and young.

We could not talk to each other but she looked at my clothes; tried on my glasses, laughing, and crossing her eyes behind the prescription lenses; twisted the earrings out of my ears, examining the pearl studs in minute detail as if she were a jeweller. She took off my watch and pressed it against her ear, nodding her head in time with the tick. She put it on her thin wrist and it hung loose and large on her small bones. She shook it up and down her arm, looking at it with her arm extended and then close up. Then she took it off and put it back on my wrist. She dropped my earrings back into my lap, got up and left to join her friends. I sat in surprised silence as she walked away. I had been under the illusion that I interested her, but to her I had been a market stall, and she was just not impressed by what was on offer.

The porters were putting their packs back on and Karma appeared on the pathway below me. Will was walking up from the fields, stowing away the threshing films that he had just taken. He arrived beside Karma. They both saw my despondent expression and the young miss sashaying back to her friends with her nose in the air.

'Are you alright?' Will asked.

'How Paradise hath fallen.' I intoned.

They looked at me and shrugged at my ranting.

We left the threshing field and walked on through the village. Sangma was a stage on from Mudh. Tall sentinels sprouting wires marked the arrival of electricity between the simple houses. But there was also a difference in this village. Apart from the colour of the blue house, the homes of Mudh had been minor variations on a theme. In contrast, Sangma boasted houses that seemed to fit a merchant class. They rose from the dusty paths with heavy stonework. Some were better kept than others with bright, clean paintwork around the windows and below the layered roofs. Others were past their prime, their whitewash fading, the red and ochre paintwork running down from their windows like bad make-up at the end of a party. Some of the window frames were carved with intricate details that had been weathered to soft silver. A couple of them even had Juliet balconies, seemingly suspended by good faith, below the roofs. They were delicate wooden structures with prettily arched uprights, but it would have been a brave man or woman who stepped out onto them without risking an ugly accident.

The village was deserted. Every man, woman and creature seemed to have moved down to the threshing field, leaving their homes silent and still. We walked away without the twitch of a window or the wave of a hand.

There was just one more rite of passage to be made before we reached the end of the walk.

Crossing rivers in the Himalayas gives a wealth of experience on its own. With smaller rivers it is usually a question of trying to leap across in one go, a move pre-empted by that cruel moment on the bank when your body begins to lurch into action but your legs will not join in the game. After several sways at the opposite bank there is usually a faint-hearted attempt which ends up with some, or most of you, landing in the freezing water amidst howls of shock and indignation. Sometimes there are rocks to try and leap at. This is even more perilous. Leaping rarely comes into it. It is more likely to be a series of the swaying attempts, with a chorus of encouragement from those smug enough to have got across before you. The rocks are fraught with danger. Some are just good old-fashioned lads that let you jump onto them with little fuss. Others have a layer of slime on them where the water turns their surface lichens into a perilous slide; you shoot across these and end up smacking down on your coccyx. Alternatively you can slip backwards ending up prostrate over the rock, clinging and winded, a pathetic, moaning limpet with scraped shins.

The rivers become more ferocious as they flow down the mountains. Bridge construction is almost impossible at this altitude. The logistics of getting materials to suitable sites are absurd. On the Indian side of the mountains there is a rash of prefabricated Bailey bridges, the Lego constructions introduced to India by the British Army. Spiti does not have many Bailey bridges, except where technical engineering is creeping in to drive roads through the valley. Instead, they have devised a series of instruments of torture for those of a nervous nature. For vertigo sufferers these methods of crossing just about spell certain death. The locals winch their animals and themselves across ravines and rivers on tight wires based on the crudest form of the cable-car system. Sometimes they just cling to a rope harness and use a sling under the animals' bellies to get them across. There might be just a chair, fastened to a wire, to haul the brave traveller across a bottomless ravine. The method that was going to carry us across this stretch of the river to the road was a shallow iron cage dragged across by a pulley system.

Amanda groaned and wailed. To her it represented stark terror. The porters look delighted. They were in for some sport.

Ella went first, merrily waving over her shoulder as she went, with a big bold smile. Amanda was wise enough to go next before her nerves and the laughter of the porters defeated her. We knotted the neck of a jersey and placed it over her head so that she could shut out the fear. I could see her mouth sucking in the material, like a hangman's victim in a sack. She crunched herself up in the cage and suffered from one side to the other. I followed, delighted by the churning water below and exhilarated by a lack of fear. Jane came next, nonchalant as I took her picture. Will was the last, cramped in the small cage, one leg stuck out, and smiling as much as his cracked, burnt face would allow. As Will hit dry land there was a whoop of delight from Amanda. Paddy had arranged for some bottles of beer to be buried in a glacial fragment beside the river. We toasted our survival in cold beer.

Karma had decided that Black and K Nau would remain on the far bank of the rushing Spiti river to be fostered by the people of Sangma. He felt that the dogs would be a drawback when we were seeking bed and board in small towns further down the line, unused to tourists with their sentimental retinues. What he had not taken into consideration was the determination of the dogs not to be deserted. He broke the news to us, that they would not be coming across, once he had us all safely on the opposite bank with bottles of beer in our hands. There was an immediate display of indignant RSPCA argument but Karma conveniently lost all knowledge of the English language. Our soppy pleading fell on deaf ears. Will began to look embarrassed as the four girls stood on the bank, waving forlornly at the expectant dogs. As we turned away with heavy sighs, they leapt into the roaring water and disappeared, immediately dragged under by the rushing current. We all gasped and waited for the bloated bodies to bob to the surface. Karma muttered and set off towards the road.

Black came up first, paddling furiously against the white water. K Nau followed after a melodramatic pause, her tail a flailing rudder. We cheered then held our breath as they were thrown around in the water; a couple of toys tossed by the river. They did make it across and lay panting on our bank looking at us with that disarming devotion that rocks even the strongest resolve. Karma was not moved. He hurried us away from the river to the chai stall where we were going to be picked up. We had reached the end of our walk.

Threshing marks the end of the agricultural year, a time of celebration when the crops come in. It is the guarantee that is going to feed the people, and their animals, through the long months of snow, when the valleys are cut off for seven months at a time.

The farming year is short. When the spring snows finally release their grip the men leave the villages to plant their fields, some of them high up among the summer pastures. The local monks lead the rite of spring into the fields with a cacophony of cymbals, drums, pipes and horns. It is in these seasonal rituals that the mingling of the early Tibetan Bön religion and Buddhism are apparent.

The Bön faith was based on animism, the belief that all things and phenomena have a soul. It was steeped in ritual and sexuality, especially around the times of sowing and harvesting, when the souls of the crops had to be placated and lauded before they could be gathered in or sown. The violent nature of some of the Bön rituals, involving sacrifice in the fields and the wild invocation of spirits, slid into the psyche of these superstitious farmers and herders. Buddhism adopted the ritual cycle of the farming year from the Bön faith, the former violent practices dwindling to a harmless musical orgy. This instrumental fusion is loud enough to shift any bad spirits that skulk into the farmers' fields, but it is non-sacrificial to fit in with the gentle Buddhist ethos.

Our end was not marked with a crash of drums and the sound of brass, but by a small chai stall on the edge of a dusty road. It was the first time that we had sat down on anything resembling a chair for several weeks. The narrow wooden benches and the scrubbed table had a luxurious permanence about them. The stallholder was delighted. Not only was he having to provide chai for twenty-five, but we were pouncing on his packets of stale biscuits with an enthusiasm that must have been rare even in this remote place.

On his ragged shelves were packets and containers. It was not easy to see exactly what they contained, but they were proof that we were back on a line of communication and transport. The stale biscuits came by road and we had now come into a part of Spiti that was more accessible than the lonely high places that we had been walking through.

Along this road came the bus that was to take us to Kaza, the biggest town in Spiti. Karma finally put his foot down. He decreed that the bus was for us, not for the dogs.

We left Black and K Nau with the chai stallholder. He seemed delighted to be the new owner of two such fine, strong animals. He had a small boy who fell on the animals with abandon, hanging on to Black's tail like a lifeline and almost swinging off his ears. The dog stood patiently while the child mauled him, resigned to his new role as a gentle family pet. K Nau was not quite as enthusiastic. If she could have pouted she would have.

This time we did have a farewell committee. The chai stallhalder obviously felt that he must show willing as we had stacked up a good bill in chai and left him with two fine dogs as a bonus. They stood outside the hut with a few other characters who had peopled the dim interior of the stall. They all waved as the rickety bus bumped us away.

Thus we closed the dog chapter of our travels. It was not a lingering moment. The farewell committee soon turned away and disappeared back into the hut.

Buses in India never go far before there is some kind of drama. We lasted about five miles, bouncing along the rocky dust road, before we all had to climb off because there was a puncture. I had already disembarked about half a mile before the puncture when the bus lumbered towards a fording place. I had leapt off with the porters ordered by Karma to lighten the load. It may have been something from the crossing that caused the puncture but it was more likely to have been the Indian predilection for driving on totally bald tyres. The bus limped from the crossing to a nearby settlement where the rest of the group piled out. A general synod of settlement elders appeared to discuss the best way to change the bus tyre. There was a lot of peering and poking at the collapsed tyre, followed by an extended period when they all stood around with their hands on their hips discussing 'ways and means'.

For a while we loitered around in case there was any chance of a quick tyre change. When this possibility proved groundless we wandered off to see what we could find. It was soft afternoon light so Will set off necklaced with cameras.

A deep gully separated the road and the rest of the settlement. As I walked along I came level with one house that was closer to the edge of the road than the others. On the roof there were two girls and a man piling up some bundles of barley to dry. When they had finished the man and one of the girls climbed down from the roof into the interior of the house. The second girl stayed, stretching her arms, bending her knees, and tucking her head into her shoulder, as she tried to relieve the strain on her back. She closed her eyes and yawned. When she opened them again she was level with me and looking right into my eyes; she on her roof in her faded flowered cotton layers, me in my climbing boots and high tech fleece on a dusty road.

While we stared everything was suspended for a moment. We were just two girls of about the same age having a good stare at each other. I was enchanted by her faded flowers, dusty hair and the way that she stretched in exactly the same way as I did. She saw a tourist, I suppose, someone from a very different place, with androgynous clothes and a mess of strange, curly hair.

I was the first to look away and that pricked the moment. Suddenly we were, once again, from two very separate worlds. She dragged her hands through her hair, conscious that she was dishevelled, and I looked down at my climbing clothes, aware of how cumbersome I looked. The moment had gone. She turned away and climbed down into the interior of the house.

'You look sad.' Will came up behind me in the road.

'She's gone.' It was a sad voice.

'Right.' I think he realised that he had bumped into a female scene. He feigned great interest in a pile of logs a little further down the road and walked away at speed.

When we got back to the bus the synod had risen to a climax. The punctured tyre had been removed and stared at with deep concentration. The spare, dragged out from the bowels of the bus in all its baldness, had been attached with a slightly casual attitude. We piled on board again.

The route into Kaza was not so much a road as a dusty, potholed track. We were driving along one side of the valley, looking across to the side that we had walked down. From the enclosure of the bus it seemed even more arid and sweeping than it had when we were walking over it.

When you are walking, you have time to adjust to the enormity of a landscape, focusing on small things in the distance and watching them grow as you slowly approach. The bus made it all move past at speed, not great speed but fast enough to turn the tiny details that we had lived with into rushing blurs. It was our first step towards divorce from the mud, the snow, the rock faces and the wet tents.

It was late afternoon by the time we came into Kaza and there was no room at the inn.

The message from Paddy that we were going to be arriving had not got through. This was the explanation given, but Karma had a different opinion. He thought that they had assumed that we would not make it over the pass in the rain, so the *chowkidar* (the rest-house watchman and guardian) had not bothered to open up the rest-house. He was safely ensconced with his family in the next village up the valley. Short of a fast runner with a message in a forked stick, there was no way of contacting him.

Sonam and Karma remained calm and headed up the road from the bus in search of a place to stay. The rest-house was battened up so there was only one alternative; the Tourist Bungalow. This title was a contradiction in terms however we looked at it. It defied being a bungalow by being built on four floors, and your average tourist would have refused to stay there. It was a badly-built lump of concrete for travellers who had nowhere else to go.

However far you travel in pursuit of the furthest tract of the globe you will always find an hirsute traveller who got there long before you did. They come ready with an armament of travel tales that allow us to leave the Mogadon bottle untouched. They are found sprawled across benches and floors from Kathmandu to Cairo, running their fingers through their long, dirty hair, inhaling deeply as you exasperate them with your lack of knowledge about their thing. They have all seen higher peaks than you, made rickshaws wheelspin with their dysentery, smoked stronger drugs than you will ever find and, most important of all, been to places so remote that the indigenous people believed them to be gods dropped straight from the heavens. They will tell you that you haven't lived as they wave a mung bean under your nose and dive at your cigarettes, pushing aside their roll-ups.

Sure enough, our travel character was ensconced in a cloud of smoke at the Tourist Bungalow. His glazed expression lit up when we trooped in. He had found a new audience.

We later discovered that he had already droned his way through the other foreign residents of the bungalow. He greeted us with a sardonic wave of his hand so as not to give away his delight at the arrival of a new crowd to bore. We were not aware of our role as lambs to the verbal slaughter. We had other things to worry about such as where we were to lay our heads for the night.

We were not welcomed with enthusiasm. Several palms had to be crossed with silver before the recalcitrance of the manager teetered towards a smile. With a little more bribery rooms became available despite the earlier cries of 'All full'. Another round of baksheesh secured us padlocks for the doors of our rooms and buckets of hot water for washing.

The guides and porters set up camp at the back of the hotel next to the kitchens. During an early search for Sonam and Karma I found the wood burner that heated the water in the backyard. This inspired us to mass hair and clothes washing that turned our rooms into Chinese laundries, filling the air with the smell of damp clothes.

It had been agreed with the manager of the hotel that Karma and Sonam would cook for us in exchange for a small reduction to the bill and a few tins of our processed cheese. He had been reluctant until a monk, who had seemed to be part of the background furniture, nodded his head to signal that the arrangement would be acceptable. The manager's opposition ended abruptly. The monk seemed to have the last word in the running of the hotel. It became apparent that the hotel was governed by the local gompa and that the monk was there as overseer. The gompa controlled not only the hotel, but a large percentage of the town, particularly anything that had any hint of being commercially viable.

I am probably naive to believe that these gompa estates are run in harmony, but there seemed to be a lack of the feudal bitterness that we associate with the early monastic stranglehold enjoyed by the European brotherhoods. Those who do not own their own land can lease it from the gompa. In return they give half of their crops to the monks. The gompas have also created a sort of education bartering system; in return for three years of gompa service the monks educate the sons of the farmers. When a tenant farmer has more than one son it is expected that the younger son will become a monk for life, provided that he comes up to the educational standard required by the gompa.

Many of the rest-houses attached to the gompas are run by the sisters of monks and the female relatives of tenant farmers. But this does not necessarily make them pious seminaries full of erudite travellers in search of enlightenment. Some of them are centres of peace and calm for those who visit. Others are about as far removed from this as you can get. It certainly does not mean that they are to be avoided. On the contrary, they are to be sought out if you want to see how a rest-house runs when it is overseen by a gaggle of girls. Perhaps it is unfair, but it seems to add fuel to the theory that the daughters of vicars run the wildest.

Will and I had a curious time at one such place in Ladakh during an earlier Indian trip. We had sought out one rest-house because we were keen to see the morning *puja* at sunrise. As the gompa was stuck out in the middle of nowhere the rest-house was our key to being able to drink in the dawn ritual.

When we first arrived, during the early afternoon, the women, who seemed to be in charge of the rest house, were lying around in shady places, looking suitably demure. We were given fairly unsavoury rooms. Will refused to consider sleeping on the mattresses or using the motley collection of blankets that looked as if they had been used as field dressings in a recent war. This did not put us off. We were in an isolated place and a roof and a door seemed to be proof that we had landed on our feet.

The calm of the afternoon had been a time of recovery for the girls. Sunset was when they came out to play. We had just climbed down from the gompa, full of the peaceful delight that you derive from being part of a working monastery for a short time. When we first got back we should perhaps have heeded the warning sign; there was still not a girl in sight. We found our way into the bowels of the kitchen in search of a cup of chai. Even this nerve centre of the household was deserted. Well, it appeared to be, until a crumpled figure uncurled from the corner, giving me short shrift for hanging around in the kitchen. This first female stirring kicked the evening action into gear. They emerged from their darkened corners with freshly plaited hair and straightened dresses. They ranged in age from very wrinkled to about seventeen. A few of the younger girls were pretty with smooth skin and warm, brown, almond eyes. As long as they kept their mouths shut they were exquisite. A smile was the letdown with the usual display of discoloured teeth, reddened by betel nuts, chewed for their mildly narcotic effect.

Will's passing interest in his female hostesses began to turn to terror during the course of the evening. I was safe enough. They laughed and shouted at me as their consumption of arak increased, but they did not make any obvious advances. Once it had been established by the girls that Will and I were in separate rooms, and not stepping out together, he was fair game. Even if we had been devoted husband and wife they probably would have had a good stab at him. He was not prepared to play and he was not going to offer up his body as a sacrifice for our easy passage through the night. There were a couple of other travellers who came to stay at the rest-house that evening. Fortunately for Will, they were both single males who seemed fairly delighted by the idea of all-night drinking and a female-instigated orgy. Once he had finished his supper, Will disappeared into his room at high speed with much banging of locks. It was not a quiet night and if the crashing and laughter was anything to judge by, the minders of the rest-house were indeed wild women of the night. I do remember a certain amount of heightened jollity on Will's part, the following morning, when we were given freehand in the kitchen because the cooks, indeed all the girls, were in no state to raise their heads from a horizontal position in a dark room. The late-arriving travellers, who had obviously been the centre-piece of the night's revelry, finally appeared at the tail-end of the morning looking as sick as parrots.

The female staff of the tourist bungalow at Kaza were thin on the ground. There was one pretty girl who could have either been the daughter or much younger wife of the front man. There was a very old woman who was part of the kitchen scene. She did not seem to have a vital role, but she was always there smiling and fiddling about with filthy vegetables. These two did not seem to be the material that the wild Ladakhi night had been made of.

Our fellow residents at the bungalow were a strange mixture. There was a pair of young Americans with bright, white teeth and glossy hair, and two boys and a girl traversing the Himalayas on a combination of bicycles and a motorbike.

The girl and one of the boys had a pattern of heading off on their mountain bikes with the dawn. The second boy was a late riser. He would eat a leisurely breakfast, and tinker with his machine a bit, before setting off in order to arrive at the next destination well ahead of his two friends. There seemed to be no animosity between the bicyclists and the biker. The pair seemed to agree that their bicycles had a much lower risk factor in the mountains. The biker had found it impossible to insure his machine due to the mountain guerrillas' penchant for big, lean machines with high revs and shiny paintwork. The boy and the girl on the bicycles felt that their silent progress across the mountains was less of an attention grabber than their friend at full throttle, roaring through the Himalayan dust.

They had had a couple of scares early on during their route along the Karakoram highway. The motorbike had broken down at an inopportune moment when its rider needed to get away from some Pakistani border guards. They had shown a little too much zeal in ripping open all his baggage and throwing it around like confetti. He had abandoned collecting it when they starting prodding at both his machine and his bottom with their kalashnikovs. He leapt on his bike, which dutifully throbbed to life, and sped down the road for a few yards until the fuel cut out.

Fortunately he had found a machine-gun-wielding border guard with a sense of humour. The other guards seemed to be about to set upon the young man to exact several pounds of flesh with their bare teeth, but the one with the sense of humour began to laugh. With this laughter the others stopped their advance, looking to see if it was the right kind of merry derision that was being poured onto the motorcyclist. They then joined him in hearty guffawing. When they got bored of splitting their sides they sloped off back to their post leaving the bemused and nervous young man trying to mend his fuel line with shaking hands. They sat and watched him from their post, offering no assistance; in fact, they seemed to be ignoring him.

After several hours they started to move around at the post again. They seemed to be involved in an argument. One of the guards left the post and headed back down to where the young man was mending his bike. The guard sprung his weapon and raised it at him. There was a cry from the guard post. The gun wielder turned around to see what was happening. Two cyclists had appeared at the post. The cavalry had arrived.

The girl produced illicit beer, American cigarettes and English chocolate. The guards were pleased but not satisfied until they were sure that they had every cigarette that the group had with them. Then the cyclists were able to claim the nervous young man and his motorbike. They were finally allowed to wheel away from the guard post in peace after one last cigarette frisk. They pushed the motorbike about fifteen miles along the uphill road before they felt safe enough to stop and resume the effort to mend the fuel line.

They all had to give up smoking for a while, until they could restock, but they felt that the cigarettes had been well spent.

Since that particular event they had made a rule that they would never get more than a couple of hours in front or behind each other. They managed to get hold of a new fuel line after waiting for three weeks in Gilgit. Eventually they had to use their last traveller's cheques to bribe a crooked mechanic to get off his backside and get the promised fuel line fast. It transpired that it had arrived a week before, but the mechanic seemed to think that they were having such a good time staying at his brother's lodging house that they did not want to leave. They paid their lodging house bill and for some oil from the mechanic, but they refused to pay for the fuel line. They sped out of town amidst a sea of waving fists.

When they told us the story they swore that they would have paid for the fuel line if they could have but they had no more money. They felt justified in not paying, having been allowed to run up an unnecessary bill. They felt that their money was circulating in the right family and they had given the mechanic so many bribes to speed the process along, that their consciences were clear.

By the time we arrived in Kaza they had been there for a few days and they had had their fill of the hairy traveller. Will ran his lens over the long lines of the motorbike and gave the girl more than a cursory glance until he saw her hairy legs. As always the biking group were planning to leave the next morning.

The American couple were too clean to be obvious travellers. When we came down for supper they were wedged in with the hairy traveller. He was giving them a blow by blow description of his recent near-death experience on the Tibetan Border. It seemed to involve a violent shepherd and his even more dangerous dog. It obviously lacked a certain amount of tension as the girl's eyes were beginning to roll and her head to bob.

Will went to the rescue, driven by the fact that the girl was pretty, even by glowing American standards; that she was attached did not deter him. After all we had travelled all over India together and we were not a couple. This meant that a pretty girl was open country unless she had a ring on her finger. It was a valiant effort and all he achieved was sighs of relief from the American couple, who slid away the moment he engaged the hairy traveller in conversation. The Americans came and talked to the rest of us while we sniggered in the corner at Will's sacrifice for a pretty face.

The couple were the archetypal US golden kids, both high fliers who had 'gotten to a stage where they needed some time out to re-evaluate their relationship and the quality of their life'. I tried to look sincere but there is something farcical about the combination of beautiful people and American pyscho-babble. They both looked about as disturbed as a double-thick shake.

They were charming, bright, and piled high with gushing enthusiasm to hear about where we had been and the people of Mudh.

This was the first time that we had been asked about the places that we had just walked through. It sparked an internal dialogue about a people who should be seen and not disturbed. Should we tell of their gentle ways and simple farms in the wild valley, or should we veil them in silence, with perhaps a passing reference to the repulsiveness of butter tea?

If you stick the label 'travel writer' on your cap and take it upon yourself to pontificate about where you have been and why, then you are between the devil and the deep blue sea. You expend time, energy, fear and delight tracking down places that have escaped the hordes, so that you can write about the wonders of far-flung purity. Then the devil on your shoulder says:

'Write, write, write, tell 'em how it is, get 'em here by the lorry load, make 'em fall in love with your words.'

While your conscience, perched on your other shoulder says:

'What gives you the right to expose them? You really think that you have the knowledge and understanding to unveil what nature and geography has protected for so long?'

You are stuck in the middle saying:

'I want to write about them but I do not want to destroy them. If I don't write then the next person who finds their way in will, and they might not understand it at all.'

Perhaps not a reasoned argument but then rationale floats away with the devil on your shoulder.

It left me feeling overprotective about a people that I had just met. But like all new lovers, infatuation had made me green-eyed.

I was rescued from my moral dilemma when the Americans established that they could not get into that bit of the valley with a vehicle. In good old blueberry muffin style they had managed to find a new jeep to take them on their whistle stop tour of the Himalayas. New jeeps are very rare in the mountains but they had paid through the nose, so that they could tick off all the places on their list and prove back home that they had 'done' India.

Will was saved by the arrival of soup. He hauled himself away from the hairy traveller who was deep into his third near-death experience. We ate without much conversation. Jane and Ella blew bidi smoke all over us and we played cards until we were all too tired to focus on the suits anymore.

Jane and I had a room opposite the lavatory. It was not a good position to be in and it was certainly not an improvement on hunching down behind a rock in the great outdoors with a good book. There was a very casual attitude towards aiming into the stinking hole, exacerbated by the fact that there was no light. That night, for the first time since I had been struck down by giardia, I could not sleep and the dragging hours were punctuated by the groan of toileteers aiming at the putrid hole in the dark.

The next morning the porters left us, piling onto another decrepit bus to take the road out of the valley back to Manali and their final pay-packet from Paddy. I am not sure if Oribadur and the other sick porter made it back. Paddy was a little vague when I asked about the two of them at a later date. They had all gone before we were woken by Karma. We did not even get a chance to say goodbye and thank-you.

We had come to the end of the first part of our journey.

[10]

THE HIGHEST VILLAGE
IN THE WORLD

K IBBER is the highest village in the world. It sits like a rook's nest on the side of the valley but is not as isolated as Mudh because the currency of Kibber is the green gold of the Himalayas – peas.

The bus driver did not want to take us up to the village. It was too high and too far. After a round of head wobbling and platitudes, he clunked the bus into gear and we crawled up the valley road. He dumped us on the edge of the village and stared in the opposite direction when we tried to thank him.

The village tumbled down the slope from the crowning glory of the gompa. Below the prayer flags was a big house and the rest of the village fanned away from it. All around were fields of bright green peas.

We split up and set off in different directions. I walked up to one of the higher fields where I found Chharringtobe. He turned out to be the richest man in Kibber and the local Mr Pea. His wealth is forged among the stalls of the Sarojini Nagar market in Delhi.

At four in the morning the air is still cool enough in the market for the stallholders to lift the mounds of vegetables without pouring with sweat. The beggars and homeless lie between the tables, motionless and angular under dirty strips of material. Some of their begging bowls have a few *paisé* (small change) or vegetables in them from stallholders keen to notch up karma points early on in the day. The market porters in their red turbans scurry among the stallholders, setting up their jobs for the day, busy and animated like a school of ants.

The fruit and vegetables begin to pour in from all the corners of India:

apples from the Kashmir and Kulu Valleys; sweet smelling, pink bananas from the south; mangoes from Mysore. There are vegetables of every shape and hue: delicate green okra, curvy gourds, fleshy onions, fat pump-kins, twined snake beans, glossy aubergines. The belching lorries bring them in from the mountains and the plains, swerving through the streets with their jolly painted cabins, their amphetamine-filled drivers hooting their way into the narrow market streets to spill their loads into the stalls. Some of these lorries come from Kibber carrying sacks of Chharringtobe's peas. They fetch a good price before they end up on the tables of Delhi as *alu matar* (spicy stewed potatoes and peas), one of the staples of the Indian diet.

Nearly all of the smallholdings in Spiti rely on subsistence farming; hand to mouth to belly and on out. They make just enough money from their excess barley to afford the seed for the next crop and the basics for their families. Some of the farmers have diversified into pea farming. It is these men who are the money-spinners of the farming communities. They are the ones who can afford to worry about the future of their valley.

Chharringtobe was squatting in the middle of one of his pea fields with his two sons by his side. The boys were in the usual mountain dress but their father wore a fake Rolex, a pair of new blue jeans with a sharp crease down the front and some RayBan Aviator sunglasses.

I stood on the edge of his field and waved to him. He beckoned me into the field. He showed me how to pick the peas, squatting on his haunches, moving along the rows of plants and testing the pods between his fingers before picking them. He gave me a pan and sent me along a row, walking beside me. Sometimes he took pods from my pan and split them in one hand, sliding the peas into his mouth in one smooth movement.

He started questioning me about farming in Europe, but my knowledge was scant and I was too embroiled in trying to get my bad knee to move along the row at the same time as practising effective quality control on the peas. He gave up and let me question him.

'Is Kibber really the highest village in the world?'

He shrugged.

'We are telling the people who come and they are believing it,' he replied.

'Where is your house in the village?'

He pointed to the big house below the gompa.

'My grandfather was building it when he married my grandmother. Her father was a pea man also. My wife is not from a pea family. Her brother is the abbot at the gompa so she is good for a wife. She small when I was marrying her, now she very big. She is carrying my wealth here.' He pointed to his stomach and laughed. The two boys laughed as well.

'How old are your two boys?'

'He seven.' He pointed to the older of the two. 'And he, I not sure, I think maybe five years.' He pointed to the younger one.

'You speak very good English, did you learn it at school?' It slipped out once more.

He laughed and the two boys laughed too.

'I am learning nothing at school. My English because the traders in Delhi are not speaking my language. I am not speaking their language. So we are speaking English.'

'Will you send your boys away to school?'

'No,' he shrieked, as I picked a series of pods that were not ripe. 'This is very bad.' He spat the bullet peas out and flicked the under-ripe pods out of my pan. 'You being careful.'

I apologised, concentrated more on the picking, and just let him talk.

'My boys must stay my boys. If they are teaching them about politics they will be wanting to see the White House. If someone telling them how big the world, they will be thinking that the pea fields are very small. Our home will be being a prison if they are thinking they want to go away. If they are staying here with the monks the fields will be seeming big.' He peeled off his sunglasses and waved them at the patches of green picked out against the dun of the mountains.

'If they are going to the cities what are they finding?' I did not answer in case he shouted at my picking again. He did not seem to want an answer.

'They will be finding girls who will be making them ill, making them scratch. They will be giving them ideas that will be making them look at our village girls in a different way. This will not be making them good pea farmers. It will be making them scratch.' He pointed at his crotch and started to laugh again. The boys joined in and Chharringtobe stopped, slapping their heads.

'If they are going to the cities they will be forgetting about *Sakadawa* (the Buddhist festival to celebrate the birth, the enlightenment and the death of Buddha). They will be forgetting their mother's eyes and how her food. They will be forgetting how to make the pea sacks strong so they are not splitting when the drivers are jumping their lorries about the roads.

'The monks are teaching them to read. If they can be writing their

[163]

names, if they can be reading contracts from the Delhi traders, that all
they are needing for farmers. That all I was knowing when my father was
dead. Then I was taking my wife and the rest I have been finding out
from that time.

'The year he was coming,' he pointed to the smaller boy, 'I was having
the greatest pea crop. Since then I am having the good fortune to have
more people working for me. I am having more time to do my things. I
am reading. Do you like the books of Mr Harold Robbins?'

I looked up to reply but he carried on.

'He is writing very good books. I am reading too a book about art. I
am very interested in the Mr Vinci of David. I am reading that David is
eighteen feet up. I do not find that very big. There are much more bigger
statues of the Lord Buddha in my country.'

He bent down and inspected my pan and gave me a nod of approval.

'My sons will be finding these things in time.'

He took the pan from my hands.

'This enough.' He helped me up from my crouching position.

I took several pictures of Chharringtobe and his two sons. They squatted
in a row amongst the peas and gave me wide smiles.

'I will be giving you my address so that you can be sending pictures of
me and my sons.' He took the piece of paper that I proffered and wrote
with a flourish.

I could not read it as it was written, so we went through a slow process
of translating his name and address phonetically. It came out as:

Mr Chharringtobe
The House
Kibber
The Himalayas

I am fully confident that the photographs did get to him when I sent them.
The Indian mail can sometimes surprise me in its ability to get letters to
the outer edge of nowhere when it fails to get them from one side of
Delhi to the other.

I sat with them for a while trying to master the art of splitting the pods
with my thumb and flicking the peas into my mouth. I was ham-fisted
about it but it made Chharringtobe and his boys laugh. I could see Jane
in the distance. She was walking down one side of the village, towards
the chai hut that stood on the edge of the fields, where the Delhi lorries
loaded the peas from Chharringtobe's fields.

They stood in a line waving when I left the field. Chharringtobe took off his glasses and waved them in the air. Then he put them back on and crouched down amongst his crop again.

Jane had been up to the gompa, but she had stayed under a tree outside while Ella and Amanda went in spiritual pursuit. We sat in the sun outside the chai stall on wobbly chairs. A very young girl seemed to be in charge of the stall, clattering about inside brewing up chai and offering us a plate of pods to split and eat. Chai and peas are a strange but delicious combination, especially when taken at the chai stall in Kibber.

Will surfaced, followed by Ella and Amanda, and the little girl in the chai stall was a whirl of arms and legs as she brewed, pushed chairs around for us and produced more pods on plates. The guides were already back at the bus and the driver was beginning to lose his temper again. He calmed down once we were all on board, and he could safely resume his original plan to take us to Key Gompa, confident that our blip of insanity in wavering from his schedule was over.

The road twisted along the high line of the valley. The bus bounced in a cloud of dust, breaking the great sections of silence, as we moved across the mountainside. Key Gompa appeared out of the rocks in front of us, clinging to an outcrop, poised between mountain and cloud.

From a distance it was small and neat with three levels of buildings, each square and whitewashed, each one stepped below the other, the corners dressed with prayer flags.

The driver dropped us at the bottom of the road that led up to the gompa. It was steep and cobbled, winding around the outcrop to the buildings. Karma knelt and kissed the ground, stretched out on his belly, then levered himself up from his prostrate position. He dusted himself down while I stared.

'Good Buddhists go to gompa like this, pilgrims go all around Lhasa like this.' He walked on ahead, still shaking the dust from his clothes.

The climb was tough enough on foot let alone the idea of doing in on my belly, yet the Tibetan believers would flatten themselves all the way to Lhasa during the month of Buddha's birthday in May. This act of *kjangchag* was witnessed by the great plant collector Frank Kingdon Ward during his travels through Tibet in 1911:

He was a ragged looking man, dirty and unkempt, as well he might be, with a leather apron over his long cloak, and his hands thrust through the straps of flat wooden clogs, like Japanese sandals. Standing up with his arms by his side, he clapped the clogs together in front of him

[165]

once, twice, then slowly raised them above his head, and clapping them together a third time, stretched himself at full length on the ground with his arms straight out in front of him. Mumbling a prayer he again clapped, made a mark on the ground at the full stretch of his arms, and rose to his feet. Then he solemnly walked forward three steps to the mark he had made, and repeated the performance; and so the weary journey went on.

The idea of *korlam*, or the circumambulation of sacred places during Buddhist high days and holidays, reflects the belief that man moves around Buddha in the same way as the planets move around the sun. To Buddhists *kjangchag* is both healthy and holy, a sort of yoga salutation in the approach to Buddha. It seemed easier for us to walk.

When we arrived upright at the entrance we were confronted by scaffolding and a battalion of workmen encrusted in white dust. They whistled and hollered at the sight of three women but Karma shepherded us past with the air of a governess. It was a pity that the front of the gompa was masked by the scaffolding, but the monks' delight in their building project for a new prayer hall and library removed the disappointment.

Key Gompa is regarded as an important monastery. Like the other major gompas of the area, Tabo and Dhankar, it is a monastery of the *Gelugpa* (virtuous) sect. This is the yellow-hatted sect of Tibetan Buddhism. It is the largest order and dates from the eleventh century. During the sixteenth century the Dalai Lama became the head of the order and the main monasteries were around Lhasa, housing between three thousand and 20 000 monks each. The other two important monasteries in the valley are Kungri and Tanguid. Tanguid belongs to the *Sakyapa* sect, an order dating from the ninth century that was designated to govern Tibet during the thirteenth and fourteenth centuries. During the latter period it was the spiritual guide of the Mongols and, in particular, Kublai Khan. Kungri is a monastery of the *Nyingmapa* sect. This is the order of the red hats, the oldest sect, founded in the eighth century and based on the esoteric teachings of Padma Sambhava.

Key is one of the important library (*kanjur-lhakang*) gompas. During its peak every monk in Spiti would pass through to draw from the knowledge of the library monks. Now it does not feel like a big monastery that was once filled with young monks drinking in knowledge from the library.

We were shown onto a small roof terrace to take off our shoes before we went into the main part of the gompa. We sat along a low wall waiting to be taken in. There were two doorways. The first one was small and covered by a door-hanging with faded colours and darkened patches from years of pushing hands. The other was resplendent in the middle of the courtyard, dressed in all its Buddhist finery.

The Tibetan Buddhists love bright colours. They wash their gompas in white and ochre with the familiar black-eyed windows. The wooden pillars that hold up the roofs and the balconies are striped in yellow, orange, red, green and blue. The woodwork is sometimes painted with delicate Buddhist illustrations picked out in gold. The poles on the corners of the building are dressed in frilled layers; flamenco dancers in the wind in rainbow stripes. When you first walk into a gompa of this design there is a feeling of arriving in a fairground, a place where children play and grow, a place where people laugh. A small boy will run across a courtyard, hotly pursued by several others and they become part of the bright scenery, filling it with flying characters.

We did not see any children at Key. There may have been some but it seemed to be a seat of advanced learning rather than a fully-fledged monastery. We were ushered from the first courtyard by an older monk with deep laughter lines around his eyes. He led us into a corridor where we sat and waited to be received, one by one, by the abbot (*khenpo*) of the gompa.

He was sitting with one leg tucked up under his bottom and the other dangling over the edge of his chair. He wore an ochre robe but he had a new woollen cardigan over the top, zipped right up to his chin. He wore a pair of good glasses and there was a black Delsey briefcase, with large silver locks, balanced on his knees. He was punching numbers into a calculator while talking to a young woman who was sitting at his feet with a baby on her lap. She was a pretty girl, dressed in a mixture of the traditional long tunic with a smart western shirt and pink cardigan. The baby could have popped out of a nappy advert. She had dark hair, olive skin and Jersey cow eyes with curling lashes. She was dressed in a pristine powder-pink babygro, and a white cardigan with little blue elephant buttons. She was surrounded by an elaborate display of toys.

I was slightly taken aback. I had not expected to find a man stooped in prayer, but neither had I expected to come into a family scene. Perhaps the woman was the abbot's sister and had dropped into the gompa to visit; but surely a sister would not sit at her brother's feet in such a submissive manner? All the questions that I had wanted to ask about faith, life and the big picture disappeared, consumed by my longing to know about his marital status.

[167]

'Hello, who you are?' His English was good and his accent even verged on a mid-Atlantic twang.

'I am with the party that you are meeting at the moment.' I mumbled.

He looked at me with a bemused expression.

'Yes?' he questioned.

'Oh, I see, you mean who am I. I am Justine Hardy and I come from London.'

'We have many Buddhists in London. Are you a Buddhist?' he asked.

'I am afraid that I'm not. Not that I wouldn't want to be. I mean I do believe in your ideals. I'm just not quite sure whether Western lifestyle can really embrace them when we spend most of our time worrying about mortgages and keeping up with the "in crowd". It just seems to conflict with all the fundamental lessons that Buddha taught. I really do not know enough to be able . . .' He held up his hand to stop me.

'You should not be sorry. I am not telling you to be a Buddhist. You will tell yourself. If you believe in something then you have more than many people.' He leant down and picked up a toy to give to his daughter or niece or whoever she was.

I realised that I had been given an audience and that it was now over. I had been another gushing tourist trying to say too much in one minute. All I really wanted to know was who the baby belonged to.

Karma had his two minutes of wisdom after me. I was sitting outside the abbot's room with a blank expression when he came out. He had a fulfilled smile.

'Um, Karma, did you see the baby with the abbot?' I asked.

'Yes.' He began to walk back towards the others, waiting in the courtyard to be taken to see the rest of the gompa.

'Was that the mother with the baby?'

'*Achchhà*, wife of abbot, mother of baby,' he replied.

He was now too far ahead for me to question him without raising my voice in the silence of the gompa.

I edged towards Ella in the courtyard.

'Did you see the baby?' I asked.

'Yes, wasn't she gorgeous.' She smiled, remembering the pretty baby.

'But he was an abbot,' I huffed.

'Vicars get married.'

She was right yet I was surprised.

An abbot does not have to take the vows of chastity that the monks take. They are not considered to be reincarnations selected for spiritual leadership. They are the more domesticated minders of the faith selected by the Buddhist Monastic Board. An abbot may take a wife and have children within a chaste society. Here was a man who was having to punish other monks for committing an act that he was allowed to pursue, with impunity, when the mood grabbed him.

Every two weeks the monks gather to recite the rules of *Vinaya* ('that which leads'). This is akin to running through the Ten Commandments, and after each rule has been chanted there is a suitable pause for anyone to admit that they have transgressed. This is when the abbot metes out punishment. The sentence of expulsion from the monastery is passed if a monk admits to having sexual intercourse, committing theft, murder, or exaggerating or misleading others about his own miraculous powers. Lesser crimes such as drinking or lying are punished by sets of rules that fall into seven groups to deal with various offences. With this power an abbot can cast a monk into darkness for committing a sexual act, while he may take a wife with the blessing of his faith. It would be difficult to accept a sentence in this 'do as I say, not as I do' situation.

I mulled over Ella's comments as we were led down into the intestines of the gompa.

We came out of a dark corridor into a room washed in sunlight and clouded by dust so that the sun shot through it in sharp, bright blocks. The cause of the dust was a thigh-high pile of manuscripts. It was being laboriously sifted through, dusted down, read, catalogued and filed into the library by a row of monks, their heads bent low over their work, trying to decipher the words in the clouds of history that came out of the mound of paper, ancient mantras from gompas in Tibet that had been sacked or burnt down by the Chinese. These dusty remains had been smuggled out by monks who had managed to get away, or they had been passed to someone who could smuggle them into Spiti.

We crouched down beside the monks to get a closer look. The pieces of mantra had been hand-painted and illuminated on black-stained parchment, the swings and loops of the words picked out in gold and silver.

As I write there is a piece of one of those mantras on the wall beside me, stuck behind a glass frame. It is a large page that has been torn in half, ripped in anger or perhaps just with age. One of the monks gave it to me. I was sitting beside him running my fingers over the letters as if it might help me to make sense of the words. He was watching me and picked up the piece of torn mantra from the pile.

'Take.' He held it out to me.

I hesitated then took it, turning it over gently in my hands. It was dry and powdery. There was a fold down the middle that had cracked the parchment. It collapsed in my hand like a butterfly. I handed it nervously back to the monk. He blocked me with his hand.

'Take.' He closed his eyes to finalise it.

'I don't think I can.'

He nodded his head and waved his hand to dismiss me. I folded the limp butterfly carefully and put it between the pages of my diary. I thanked him. He nodded, smiling, and returned to his work.

When I look at it beside me on the wall it brings back the dust and slanting sunshine in the library, and the monks, bent over their work, preserving what remains of rescued Tibet.

The last room that we were allowed into was the kitchen. The only source of light in the room was from a small window set high in the wall above the door. It threw a spotlight onto the blackened clay hearth that was the centre-piece of the room. The surrounding shelves held serried ranks of brass and copper cooking pots, serving dishes, ladles, kettles and food jars, all burnished until they glowed in the diluted sunlight. There were two monks standing guard over their domain. They let us hover at the edge of the room, but we were not allowed to wander among the pots and pans. They herded us towards a line of five chairs that stood against one of the walls, well away from the central action of the kitchen.

We sat in a line as if we were waiting for a bus, slightly wary on our frail chairs. The monks smiled and offered us tea. We sat with the cups balanced on our knees and tried to take in the details of the kitchen in the gloom. Karma chattered to one of the monks but the rest of us were silent.

We left Key Gompa and the workmen shouted and jumped around the scaffolding as we went past again. Walking back down the road we passed the outhouses of the monastery, the storage huts and sheds that had been put up to house the workers when they came down from their scaffolding. At the bottom of the rock outcrop were the gardens where the monks grew a few vegetables and medicinal plants to supply the gompa. It was a self-contained settlement, except that there seemed to be no sign of the dead, no graveyard or mausoleum of any kind.

Amanda was walking beside me. I asked her whether the Buddhists buried their dead, or were they all burnt, in the same way as the lamas, in the urns that became *stupas*. She did not know, but it seemed unlikely as the valley would be prickled with clumps of *stupas* if every body was marked with one.

Sonam was admiring the vegetable garden.

'Do Buddhists bury their dead?' I asked.

[170]

He stared at the vegetables for a while as if he was trying to find an answer.

'Buddhists do sky burial.'

Buddhists see death as an error that can be overcome by those who have entered through the *Bardo's* 'gates of the undying'. For many people this is an area of Buddhism where a curtain of confusion falls.

'Buddhists do not die.' Sonam smiled.

'Of course they die,' I said.

'Buddha say no need to die. If we die, we have done bad things. Mara, the death god, finds us when we want money and things. He punishes greed with death. Yama, the judge of dead people, makes his mind where you go; to heaven or hell. Buddhists have *Bardo* to help them fight Yama.'

Ella had told me a bit about the dreadful Yama and the *Bardo Thodol*, *The Tibetan Book of the Dead*.

Yama sits in judgement of the dead, a horrifying figure depicted in dark blue-black with a buffalo head, holding a spine and skull as a club, dangling a noose from his hand. He bestrides a fire-breathing buffalo, thrusting his enormous erection towards the animal's head, portraying a foul sexual excitement in his role as harbinger of death.

Karma and Sonam believe that there is a time between the moment of physical death and real death when Yama can consign them to an eternity of rebirth. The words of the *Bardo* coax them through this time, teaching the ways to break the cycle. Ella had told me about the *Bardo's* advice on womb blocking; how to stop the dying soul from being forced into another womb to begin a new life. The book tells the reader to bar their entrance with deep meditation and breathing, leaving behind all thoughts of envy and greed, and thinking deeply about the spiritual mentor, the Father and Mother.

Whatever the *Bardo* teaches, the body does give up and burial does have to take place.

I chased after Sonam.

'What happens with sky burial?' I asked.

'Astrologer decides if the body to go to earth, air, fire or wood. Burning is for lamas as not so much wood up here. Wood is when body is left in trunk of a tree. Water is for children or beggars. In the mountains it is sky burial.' He waved his hand at the huge horizon.

'But how do you have sky burial?'

Sonam thought for a moment. He squatted into the sitting position with his arms straight at his sides.

'Wrapped like this. Taken up to high place and cut up in special way.

[171]

Bones are ground to *tsampa*. All is for the birds. If they leave much it is bad sign.' He straightened up again.

'Have you seen one taking place?'

'Not for seeing. In Tibet tourists are watching and making trouble. Buddhists do not stand on graves of others. They are not wanting people watching for bad reasons.' He gave me one of his big smiles and headed back to the bus.

That evening we wandered the streets of Kaza. The street market was still open and there was a choice of dried apricots for sale, some soft pale orange, others wizened, dark brown bullets. The latter were considered to be more of a delicacy as the extended drying process intensifies the flavour. I was so determined to get to the taste that I split my tooth on one of the stones. I howled and held the expensive cap aloft. Nobody seemed particularly interested and it did not hurt much, so the moment passed.

We found some of the tiny backstreet shops where Will and I pounced on a dusty supply of chocolate, proudly laid out under a glass case so that it could sweat nicely in the sun. We paid huge amounts and even though it was stale and tired it was worth it for the brief moment that it lasted. Any sympathy I had hoped to glean for my tooth disappeared as I wolfed the chocolate with no sign of pain.

I walked up to Kaza Gompa just before sunset. The first courtyard was empty. The evening *puja* was beginning and the sound of chanting, cymbals and gongs hung in the captured air of the courtyard.

I sat down on the steps below the prayer hall to listen to the *puja* falling out through the open doors. The light was playing games with the ragged horizon beyond the roofs of the courtyard, turning the peaks to molten razors against the washed sky. At the outer corners the skirted prayer flags danced in the wind, lifting their coloured dresses like cock-teasing dancers in the fertile air. It was like a moment out of the Bible. In the still there could have been a silent voice:

'And the lion will lie down with the lamb.'

THE OCHRE MONASTERY

T HERE were ten flies crawling up the border guard's arm and he seemed to be totally oblivious to them. It was not until one landed on his nose, and made its way down to his moustache, that he raised his hand to brush it away. The fly was bullish and no sooner had he dropped his hand than it alighted on his face again. This time he ignored it.

I was so fascinated by the journey of the flies over his body that I found it almost impossible to concentrate on what the border guard was saying. It was the third time that we had been made to stop since we had left Kaza a couple of hours earlier that morning. On the previous two occasions we had all been made to get off the bus and line up while they shuffled through our permits and passports.

Indian border posts involve an etiquette that unfolds like a lumbering dance. None of the partners dance to the same tune, but none are going to change to suit the others. The border guards all seem to be members of the same family or linked by some genetic code; tidy in a ramshackle Indian fashion in tired uniforms, bulled and pressed to survive beyond their natural life. They all have moustaches and they ask the same questions.

Turning to Will, they start by asking me:

'Is this your husband?'

Will and I in unison:

'No.'

'Where is your husband?'

'I do not have a husband.'

'Your husband is dead?'

'No, I have not been married.'

'This is most strange.' There usually followed a great deal of head nodding and more concentrated flicking through my passport as if they were searching through the pages for some clue to my single status.

This treatment was by no means exceptional. There were four of us; all single. By the time we reached the third checkpoint there was a flood of relief when it transpired that only I would have to go and talk to the border guard.

He had only a passing interest in my marital status. I was prepared for the usual nuptial barrage and was about to launch into my practised speech, but it never really came. I think this made me a little indignant.

'You are from London,' he stated with my passport open in front of him. 'My cousin is in London.' He looked at where my profession was marked as a journalist. 'You will know him. He is working with a newspaper and he is living in Wembley. He is a very good man.'

He seemed offended that I did not know his cousin, so I tried to make amends by complimenting him on the tidy order in his guard tent. This cheered him up.

'You are going to the gompa?' he asked.

'Yes, we are.'

'The Dalai Lama is coming.' He snapped my passport shut and gave it back to me with the other four. Then he shooed me out of his guard tent before I could quiz him about the visit of His Holiness.

In 1995 Tabo Gompa will celebrate its millennium and the Dalai Lama is to join the monks in celebrating this monastery's passage through history. Tabo is ranked as one of the holiest places of Tibetan Buddhism. Rinchen Tsangpo, the great translator, has his *stupa* here. In about 970 the bright young Tibetan monk Tsangpo was sent to India by King Khorde of Guge. This king was an extraordinary man who renounced his throne to become the Royal Monk, Yeshe Ö. He maintained much of his authority as a sovereign while taking up his monastic role. In this way he became one of the strong influences in spreading Buddhism into Tibet at this important time in the gestation of the faith. Yeshe Ö is believed to be the founder of Tabo.

We arrived at Yeshe Ö's gompa in the heat of the day. Tabo is not like other gompas. It lies on the valley floor and the surrounding village seems to be part of the monastery, the one running into the other. The first impression was of a group of giant African anthills. The main part of the gompa does not have any of the whitewhashed walls or bright colours that leap out from other gompas. It is built of sand and rock and the feeling is of the desert; sometimes a desert in bloom, when the courtyard brims with novice monks, rushing like ochre marbles on a tilting tray; at other times a silent desert, empty and calm.

We were dropped at the gompa rest-house. For the first time Will was forced into a dormitory with all the girls. We had a long room with shuttered windows that looked out over the gompa and we spread ourselves among the line of beds, each of us making a little room around ourselves in response to this first grab at sleeping space for weeks.

Then we went to meet the monks. It was the bright white afternoon light when we walked in through the monastery gates. To our left were the living quarters of the monks and novices hidden behind a high wall. In front of us were the main buildings of the gompa, the same ancient *du-khangs* (assembly halls) that had been built in the tenth century. The courtyard was dotted with eight separate buildings, the main one being a huge sand-coloured *stupa* rising from stone steps up to a voluptuous bulb. This turned out to be Rinchen Tsangpo's *stupa*. Behind this was the main *du-khang*, a low, flat-roofed building, simple and unadorned. We knew that it housed some of the most important pieces of Buddhist art that have survived intact.

In the shadows of the walls of the *du-khang* a large group of young women sheltered from the heat. They had just been celebrating the *puja* of female fertility.

Most of the women had a baby strapped to their back or were in the advanced stages of pregnancy. They were all dressed in their equivalent of Sunday best; bright, flowered tunics, with busy shawls or cropped silk jackets, thick ropes of seed pearls with turquoise and coral; their hair scraped back and tied with fresh ribbons. The older women did not seem to have made quite as much of an effort with their appearance. Their tunics were dirtier and there was a scattering of grubby cardigans among the floral landscape. The younger ones looked expectant and freshly washed. They all had similar faces, round and high-cheeked with dark almond eyes and olive skin. One girl in particular stood out. She had a longer face than the others. Her cheekbones and nose were sprinkled with freckles and her lips were fuller and gentler than the thin, chattering ones of the other women around her.

The group was lined up, according to height and being photographed by one of the senior monks. He was squatting in the middle of the court-yard, trying to angle himself out of the direct sun. His robes were hoicked up so that they were not in his way as he photographed. The women were giggling and nudging one another. From where I was standing it was hard to tell, but it did look as if they were trying to see under the monk's robes.

We asked if we could join the photographic session. Ella and Amanda posed with the women. There was a great deal of laughter as they prodded the two girls' flat stomachs. They smiled sweetly and tried to look at home amongst the gaggle of fecund women.

I asked the pretty girl with freckles whether I could take her picture. She blushed and hid her face behind her hands, but all the others pushed and cajoled her. She let me take the picture, holding her hands protectively over her extended stomach and looking up shyly into the camera like a young Diana Spencer.

The group were about to be given a free lunch by the monks, so the novelty of the white tourists wore off quickly. We were appointed a young tutor monk to take us to see the ancient wall-paintings in the main *du-khang*.

There seemed to be no windows and, after the bright sun, we were plunged into darkness. As our eyes got used to the gloom we could see the stucco protectors on either side of the door watching over those who passed by. They had wild, snarling faces, their cruel plaster lips pulled back over sharp teeth and their blank eyeballs rolling away from each other. They were reminiscent of the wild warriors of the Chinese Water Margins, their arms wielding weapons at those who dared pass with an unclear conscience.

From the darkness we came into the main part of the *du-khang* palely lit by a skylight. All around us the walls sprang into life and colour with a frieze of paintings that stretched away around the length of the building. This great painting seemed to be divided into three separate layers. The first was made up of a continuous series of anecdotal paintings. Several of these scenes showed crowds of monks paying homage to a smiling character on a lotus throne. Our young guide told us that the smiling man was the depiction of Jangchub Ö, the grandson of Yeshe Ö. He became a royal monk like his grandfather and is attributed with extensive renovations at Tabo in the mid-eleventh century. The second layer was an array of thirty-two seated stucco figures, most of them in the lotus position caressing their rounded bellies, fingering delicate blossoms or waving their slim fingers while smiling serenely at the delicate painted goddesses behind them. The upper layer was made up of devotional paintings.

Our guide pointed to the characters in this third layer. He picked out the ones that he thought might be familiar to us. There was Avalokiteshvara, the patron saint of Tibet, his eleven wise faces framed by a great fan. As I got closer to the painting I realised that the fan was made up of his myriad arms. The monk then pointed to a nearby Green Tara, the consort of Avalokiteshvara. She was smiling with a verdant sexuality; a symbol of female fertility and power sitting on a moon disc and lotus flower, her right leg extended with her delicate foot coquettishly resting on another lotus blossom. Her eyes seemed to be gliding sideways towards her lord, Avalokiteshvara, trying to focus on one of his many hands. Our monk pointed to the paintings of Buddha. He showed us the contrast between the other characters, their figures full of movement, their heads turning and their navels stretched in twists and turns, and the still calm of the Buddhas, staring from the walls with expressions of understanding or smiling wisdom.

We stood and stared, trying to drink in the importance of the paintings that we were seeing, conscious of the beautiful colours, faded by nearly a thousand years but protected by the darkness. We were not allowed to take pictures. It seemed suitable that we could not flash at these ancient paintings and statues and just slot them away in albums. Now, trying to remember the pieces in detail is like putting a jigsaw puzzle together with my eyes half closed. There were so many images that they have become a constantly changing canvas of smiling faces, lotus positions and floating robes.

We came out of the weak, dusty light of the chapel into the main part of the *du-khang*. Before we could wander away to different parts of the hall the monk held out a donation box towards us. We all looked embarrassed as we fished into our pockets. He watched us put each note into the box until he was satisfied that we had given enough. Then he retreated, signalling that we could now wander at will.

The central shrine table was surrounded by a combination of high art and the contents of a child's toy box. A gold screen above the table was studded with precious stones, pearls, rubies, emeralds, turquoise, coral and lapis lazuli. The shrine shimmered in the light of several rows of small butter lamps that gave off a thin cloud of dark smoke as they burnt. The focal piece was a photograph of the Dalai Lama, framed in a deep, gilded setting, smiling from behind his glasses. The cloth on the shrine table brought back the room of the young monk in Mudh; a shiny pink thing more suitable for a suburban housecoat topped with a set of curlers. Resting on the edge of the cloth was an array of ugly plastic flowers, their rude purple and orange petals greyed by dust and dirt. One of the table-legs had broken and was propped up by a powdered milk tin.

I sat on a low bench in front of the shrine, trying to get into the lotus position. I rested my hands, one on top of the other, in my lap with the thumbs touching as we had just seen in so many of the paintings. All that I could manage to focus on was the smiling Dalai Lama, the dirty plastic flowers and the powdered milk tin.

The monk was still waiting by the entrance when we left. He lingered with us as we talked in the shade of the prayer hall, blinking in the bright sun.

'Do you collect enough money for the upkeep of the gompa?' I asked.

He peered into the slit in the wooden collection box before answering.

'This is for millennium celebration. We paint and wash and make things new.' He smiled at the prospect.

'I hope we have given enough.'

'We all give what we think is right. Many people do not give much. Some Americans came here not long ago. They were big and gave much money. Some people do not have much if they travel. You are kind,' he said.

He started to laugh.

'The Americans gave much for it was hot day and they were giving much to stay in the soft of here.' He pointed back into the dark interior of the prayer hall.

'We will make it good for His Holiness Dalai Lama when he come back,' he continued.

'Has he been here before?' Will asked.

'Yes. His Holiness here in 1959 when he escape from Tibet.' He straightened with pride.

There was a hint of an apocryphal story.

In the Dalai Lama's former bedroom in the Potala Palace outside Lhasa his clock and calendar have been left at the time and the date of his departure from the city on 31 March 1959.

The Chinese had been losing their patience for several weeks. They had been trying to get the young Dalai Lama to attend a dance show at the Chinese military headquarters in Lhasa. The people of Lhasa had sensed the danger in the invitation and they had surrounded the Dalai Lama's residence, Norbulingka, just outside the city.

As the military movements of the Chinese against the crowd protecting this one young man heightened, he consulted his oracle and another form of divination known as *Mo*. Both sources confirmed that he should stay and continue to keep a dialogue open with the Chinese. Then he received a letter from the Chinese generals asking him to mark on a map where he would be in the palace as the People's Liberation Army (PLA) were going to attack the crowd and shell the Norbulingka. By marking his residence the Chinese artillery could be briefed not to aim at it. The Dalai Lama realised the immediate danger that his people and he were in. Once again he consulted the oracle and *Mo* and this time they both warned 'Go! Go! Tonight'.

For the last time he went to his personal shrine to present a *khata*, a length of white silk given as a devotional greeting or farewell. The Dalai Lama gave it as a token of farewell but with the intention to return.

He left Norbulingka at ten o'clock in the chill March night air, dressed in heavy, unfamiliar clothes with a rifle slung across his back and his trademark glasses hidden in his pocket. Without his glasses his departure was even more unfocused and confusing. He passed, with a couple of soldiers and his commanders, through the sea of Tibetans guarding Norbulingka. The small party carried on as if performing an on-the-spot inspection and the crowd let them pass without recognising their holy leader. They crossed the river away from Lhasa without the Chinese managing to stop them.

The Dalai Lama, his family and retinue climbed away from their city until they reached the Che-La Pass. A groom stopped the pony that His Holiness was riding and told him that it would be the last view that they would have of Lhasa.

'The ancient city looked serene as ever as it lay spread out far below. I prayed for a few minutes before dismounting and running on foot down the sandy slopes,' he wrote in his autobiography.

A few days later the escape party received news that the PLA had opened fire on the Tibetans outside Norbulingka and shelled the residence. With his hopes of negotiating with the Chinese disintegrating, he realised that he would have to exist in exile. In this saddened state he contracted bad dysentery and limped out of Tibet.

It was at this time that our monk told us the escaping Dalai Lama arrived at Tabo.

There was just one vital flaw in his story. The Dalai Lama's escape route from Lhasa to India actually passed over the border just east of Bhutan, about a thousand miles south of Tabo along the Tibetan Border.

None of us questioned his story. He told it with such fluency that it was easy to believe. It was not until I poured over a map at a later date that I realised the improbability of the tale.

He was a great talker. He seemed to have travelled quite a lot and he was keen to tell us his tales. He told us about the lakes outside Tokyo and about a Benedictine monastery in Italy near Siena where he had picked olives and eaten pasta. It was quite a battle to get him on to another subject until it was established that he taught the novices philosophy.

I asked him how a typical day for him ran.

'I wake them for the morning *puja*. In the hot time they sleep outside their rooms so it is easy to wake them. If they do not wake there is water thrown on them.

'After the *puja* they wash by the pump in the yard. They hear the noises that the monks make and they try to do the same.' He cleared the phlegm from his throat with a gutteral roar and spat into the dust to demonstrate: 'Like this.' He laughed.

'We have to teach them all things. We are a mother and a father for them. Sometimes the very young boys are sorry that they are not with their families. We have to teach them that we are their new family. For some they only stay three years so it is not so bad. For a chosen lama it is hard. He must understand that the rest of his life is so different.' He rubbed both his hands over his shaven head.

There were a couple of little white scars on his scalp. I asked him how he got them.

He read my expression as concern.

'They cut me when they shave me.' He laughed again and shook his head.

'No, no, not true. When I was young we were always fighting and being cut. You will see the novices. They are all cuts and bangs. You will come back later. I will be teaching philosophy near to here.' He pointed towards the *du-khang*. 'Goodbye.' He walked away to the monks' living quarters on the other side of the courtyard.

It was the hottest part of the day so we sought out the cool of the dark kitchen and dining room. They were both quiet and empty apart from a single monk clearing up the debris from the ladies' lunch in an unenthusiastic manner.

The outer door of the kitchen opened onto another courtyard. There was a single, sparse tree in the middle and a limp donkey stood in its narrow lines of shade. Several chickens were scratching around the door to the kitchen, one of them was stretched out at full length in the dust, her wings flattened away from her body to try and cool her down. There were a few wooden milking buckets near the donkey that looked as if they were used regularly, the wood dark and lustrous from the milk fat. But the donkey was a jack and no milk yielder. The kitchen monk pointed up the valley to the higher pastures and muttered about yaks and dzos. The latter were once considered to be the humbler version of the yak, being a cross between female yaks and cattle, until the day when the dysentery-stricken Dalai Lama escaped over the Tibetan border on the back of a dzo.

The pasture where the yaks and dzos were grazing was framed by a dazzling silver anachronism in the monastic surroundings. Set high on a platform above the roof of the kitchen, above the wooden milking buckets and the *tsampa* grinding stone, was a solar heating system. The kitchen monk looked up at it and shrugged.

'Hot water for abbot and *Geshe*.' He ducked back into the cool shadows of the kitchen.

Perhaps it is the presence of a *Geshe* at Tabo that has merited the sophisticated heating system. Only the major gompas claim the right to the attendance of a *Geshe*, the most advanced Buddhist qualification that can be gained within the monastic system. Tabo has Sonam Wangdui from Kongpo, a region next door to Central Tibet and Lhasa. He is regarded as the fount of knowledge. For his years of study he is honoured with hot water whenever he needs it.

As the most intense heat of the day began to retreat, the boys started to appear from their shadowy corners. The courtyard filled with dust, ochre and the sound of children shouting and laughing. Will came out with his tripod and cornered a few of them before they went in for their afternoon lessons. It was a strange sight; the small boys in the dark red robes against the pale sand background, with Will bent like an elastic giant over his tripod. Some of them were sitting on the ledges of the *stupa* watching the action below. They jeered down at some smaller boys fighting in the dust until their dark hair was grey from the ground. A bell rang and the courtyard was empty.

They were all lined up in the shade of the main *du-khang*. Each one of them had a wooden drawing-board. They wiped the surface with some oil on a piece of cloth then sprinkled dust from the courtyard onto the board. This gave them a surface to draw through. Their heads were bent low over their work, lower teeth working at lips and tongues poking out through serious tight lips, as they tried to duplicate the illustration of Buddha that they had in front of them. They rested their palms on small strips of wood so that they did not press down onto the fragile dust surface and destroy the work that they had already done. The drawings were built up from the framework of a grid to give the eyes the statutory distance, the nose of the Lord Buddha the right length, the lips the suitable fullness, the lashes the correct curl.

I sat above them on a wall, watching as they drew. Some of them found it easy, just letting their drawing sticks flow between the graphic lines.

Others found it hard, struggling over each line, drawing and redrawing, trying to rub away errors and leaving dull patches through the dust. One boy just below me seemed to find it easier than the rest. He had finished his drawing when most of the others were still trying to map out the main bulk of their task. He flicked his robe from his shoulder, draping the long end over his head to protect his shaved scalp from the sun. I smiled at him as if to compliment him on his drawing. He looked back at me, unmoved, and then yawned. I pulled my knees up, slightly embarrassed by being made to feel like a gawping fool. The boy's neighbour nudged him and they both looked up at me with wide, radiant smiles. I felt triumphant until I realised that the nudge was going down the line and that some of the smiles were turning to smutty laughter. They were looking straight up my shorts.

I retreated to the other side of the courtyard where there was a philosophy lesson in progress. These boys seemed safer subject for attention as their eyes were secured to their texts. The monk who had taken us around the *du-khang* was teaching. The lesson came to an end and the novices scattered across the courtyard to a small door in the wall. Beyond was their home, otherwise known as the Serkong Buddhist School and Hostel, as proclaimed on the board above the front gate.

The monk who had been teaching, beckoned to us:

'Come.'

Jane and I followed him like sheep. The others had disappeared to different parts of the gompa; Ella and Amanda in pursuit of the abbot and Will to take more snaps.

The doorway led into a garden of flowers, a sea of pink and white cosmos and bright sunflowers. Between their heavy bent blooms, the boys rushed past to their rooms, most of them smaller than the plants, dwarfed by the large yellow heads craned towards the sun.

We sat on the day beds around the edge of the courtyard and watched the ochre robes spinning past the sunflowers and scuttling up and down the ladders that led up to the balconies where they slept. They paid little attention to us; they all seemed to be full of the purpose of where they were going.

At the far end of the courtyard was the residence of the senior monk in charge of the school. Steps led up out of the flowers to a jaunty balcony painted predominantly the same colour as the sunflowers. There was an overall feeling of escapism; the bright colours and flowers after the flat, ancient architectural landscape in the main part of the gompa.

The young monk had been standing next to us while we sat and stared.

He wandered away towards the bright yellow windows at the top of the stairs. So we were left to just sit and watch the evening unfold.

Our field of vision comprised three layers; the first, the haze of flowers; the second, the bright paintwork of the wooden cloisters and balconies around us; the third, the raw rock behind which the mountains soared away from the valley.

There was one novice who was motionless in the rush of the others around him. He lay on the balcony on his day bed, his thin, brown legs crossed where his robe had slid away. He was reading, but I could not make out the title from where we were. He was absorbed by his book to the extent that he had shut out the noise and movement all around him as other boys ran past, bumping into his day bed in their haste.

When the courtyard was silent again we left the boy to read alone and went back into the main part of the gompa. The evening light was the colour of a blood orange, pitted with flecks of gold. Will was in front of the main door into the gompa courtyard. It was open to the huge landscape beyond; a great wooden double door weathered to a rich mahogany colour. Will was motionless. He was waiting, masked by the long shadows from the *du-khang*. A novice in ochre, with a dirty yellow jacket over the top of his robe, crossed the courtyard towards the door. For a moment he stopped and looked around. He saw neither Will in the shadows, nor Jane and me in the smaller doorway to the hostel. He stuck his head out through the door and then banged it shut, shooting the bolt home as if he was shutting out the marauding hordes. Will clicked and captured him.

They were building around Tabo. The little town was playing host to a crowd of builders and engineers. We had not noticed them during the day but they came out at night to make merry after their dusty day on the roads.

Jane and I had taken a detour back to the rest-house in search of the sole postbox in Tabo. The tiny post office was battened down for the night but there were two youths loitering with intent outside, basking in the last gentle sun of the day. They both spoke very good English and it transpired that they were not labourers but a contract manager and a bridge engineer. One of the first facts that they fired at us was the extent of their further education, indeed they seemed to be awash with degrees of various colours and varieties. They asked us to a party that they were about to embark on. As they seemed so erudite we felt that it would be churlish to refuse.

It was not a wild party. It was not much of a party at all. There were the two of them, one of their friends, Jane and me. We sat in a small dark room, lit only by one small window and the dying sun. They made us some tea over a camping stove and they all smoked almost as much as they talked. They were very polite and broke into Hindi only when they were too excited to get the message across in English. They all had tiptop university degrees. In fact most things about them seemed to be tiptop; their clothes; their jobs; the Bombay film industry, especially the busty, hip-wiggling stars that it spewed out; but the most tiptop thing of all was the fact that they would be leaving the Spiti Valley soon to go home for a holiday. This was an outlook that I had not been prepared to find. To us Spiti was a rare Buddhist cupping bowl that we had managed to climb into against the odds. To these young men it was a remote outpost where they had been sent, against their will, to build roads and bridges to bring the outside world in. They did not want to talk about the gompa or the monks. They wanted to know if we had been to a Madonna concert and whether her pubic hair was the same blonde as the famous mane that she sported. We left before the conversation got any more risqué.

It was now almost dark so we walked back through the gompa to avoid finding any more road contractors in party mood. The hum of mantras came from the old shrine next to the *du-khang*. A pile of dusty shoes was piled up outside the door, discarded in a hurry as the latecomers rushed to the *puja*. Their voices carried out into the courtyard, rising and falling with the drum and the cymbals. Above their mantras came the buzz of a transistor radio; as the mantras rolled, a radio advertisement starring Miss India gave us a rundown on 'Qwality Shoopolisssh'. A latecomer bolted past us, throwing his shoes onto the pile and sliding across the polished floor to take his place. The monk leading the mantras stopped for a moment before clearing a lump of phlegm from his throat, then he resumed the rhythm as night fell. This was our last night in Spiti. We sat up after supper playing cards, trying to hang on to the evening as if it might go too fast if we stopped playing. Jane won easily and I went to the end of the dormitory to sleep, irritated that I had lost so badly. The town was silent except for one dog barking at the moon.

Karma woke us early so that we would have a chance to go back into the monastery before we had to leave. By the time we had eaten breakfast and packed, the monks had finished the early morning *puja* and the work of the day had begun.

The air was cool and the sun had not yet burnt through the early morning mist that had risen from the valley. A line of the youngest novices were carrying raw window frames over to the new prayer hall that was being built beside the hostel. The smallest boy was at the back, weighed down by two frames. He was carrying them balanced on his shoulders with his head through the centre of the frames. I called out to him and he turned around. As he turned the first sun came through the mist and he was framed three times over; once by the mountains behind him, then by the glow of the sun behind his head and finally by the raw wood of the frames he was carrying. I smiled and waved. He smiled back and turned to catch up with the end of the line.

I sat in the main courtyard outside the *du-khang*. Karma's voice carried into the quiet, shouting to the bus driver to help them with the loading. The bus shuddered and choked to a standstill; then the driver started shouting back at Karma. Will and Jane were on the other side of the courtyard by the big door. They were calling out to me to hurry as the bus was leaving soon. In the far corner of the courtyard was the pile of window frames that the novices were moving to the new prayer hall. Two boys had been standing guard over the frames, doling them out to the carriers. Now that the line of boys had gone, these two were tumbling in the dust. As I got up to leave they caught sight of me. One of the boys got up and straightened the fall of material over his thin legs. His puppy-wrestling companion flicked his robe over his shoulder and walked away. The first boy shook like a dog, producing a cloud of dust. He picked up a book from beside the pile of frames. I recognised him as the boy from the hostel balcony, lost in his reading. He came towards me, holding out the book.

'Do you read the books of Julian Barnes?' asked the eight-year-old novice, showing me his copy of *Flaubert's Parrot*.

'I've read some of them, but I am afraid I find them rather difficult to understand.'

He put his head on one side and wrinkled his brow.

'Good, I do not understand too.'

EPILOGUE

WE ended our journey where it had begun; drinking Darjeeling tea from Reggie's Limoges at Chapslee in Simla. The sugar lumps were in a heavy silver pot; teaspoons tinkled on fine china; there were tiny bunches of hand-embroidered forget-me-nots on the linen tablecloth, and one of Reggie's golden labradors was edging towards the plate of scones.

Will was laughing with his head thrown back and Paddy's long legs were hanging over the generous, rolled arm of his wicker armchair. He had just been amusing us with another story about an early love triangle involving a colonel's wife and his own rapid exit from the regiment. Amanda was trying to decide whether to put apricot or strawberry jam on her scone; Ella was picking at the wicker of her chair. We had made a mental leap from the courtyard of Tabo to Reggie's homemade scones. Part of us was slightly numb, still trying to let all the things that we had seen roll over us.

Paddy was delighted that we had not been washed away with the floods. He had been worried that the carefully planted beers might have ended up as fuel for the search party rather than to quench us.

The cedar tree spread low over the edge of the terrace, as it does in a thousand Old Rectory gardens across England. The difference is the sheer peaks that rise on the horizon, heralding the gateway of the High Himalaya. Chapslee is the time trap between the two worlds of the Ochre Border and the West; a vacuum where it is possible to melt them together; the smiling monks with our metropolitan mayhem.

Reggie was our catalyst in this go-between state at Chapslee. He is equipped with a mixture of strength and wisdom spiced with dry wit. He once sent me an article about his house in which he was described as looking as if he had been 'born in his red leather punjabi slippers'. Reggie had circled it in rude red and had written: 'Rubbish, I was born with bare feet.' When he walks into a room he has the look of a warrior rajah, with a large curling moustache and deep, dark eyes, but he has his hands in the pockets of his cardigan and his feet are either shod in highly athletic gym shoes or the signature red slippers. His voice is quiet and gentle. He knows much about the remnants of the Raj.

His grandfather Charanjit Singh, the Raja of Karputhala, bought Chapslee from John Stanley Ker in 1938 and shipped in his collection of extraordinary antiques from his former residence down the road, Chadwick at Summer Hill. A relation of John Ker's, Mrs Montagu, became a part of Chapslee even after John Ker had sold the house. She was born in India in 1892 and spent the whole of her life there, apart from a brief trip to England where she married for a bet. The marriage lasted only two weeks. When she reached her dotage, Reggie and his wife built her a cottage down the road from Chapslee. People came to visit her and she sang in her sweet voice, complained about the lack of suitable young subalterns to keep her company and talked to her African Grey parrot about the nightly balls and parties of her youth. When she died Reggie adopted her parrot. He speaks of her with the same reverence that he gives to his descriptions of his grandfather's pieces, some of them bought from the Doge's Palace in Venice.

He asked us how we had found Spiti and we all gabbled away. Paddy and he sat and listened attentively as we described the monotony of the rain and the horrors of TB.

While I was trying to describe this place I realised how difficult it is to translate what we had seen into the context of the outside world. My words sounded lavish and glossy for a place that is so uncluttered and simple. Reggie told us how he had watched the mountains change as the tourists had increased. I sat looking mournful at the thought of Spiti joining the television rush into the twenty-first century.

'But it will change; we all need to go on changing or we get lost,' he said.

I climbed up Jakhoo Hill above Chapslee. It is a steep rise above Simla to a temple at the top dedicated to the Hindu monkey god, Hanuman. As you climb the sacred hill, grey langur monkeys rush at you baring their teeth, and retreating only when they are assured that they have really put the wind up you. They snatch food from your hands and languish in their elevated position as divine guardians of the temple. The Indian tourists totter up and down in their tight shirts and floating saris; the girls somehow managing the steep climb in high heels. They collapse at the top around the chai stall, content that they have worked for their karma points.

I managed to find an empty grass bank away from the temple. It had a view right down the ridge that Simla is built on. Beneath me were the rabbit warrens of the bazaar where Kipling's Kim ran. Above this was the strange English juxtaposition of spired Christchurch and the suburban promenade of The Mall looking down their noses at the alley-ways of stalls and smells of India.

It was sunset and lights were beginning to come on along the ridge, turning the dirty streets and the muddle of generations into a thread of light decorating the mountain crest. Above Simla rose the mountains, absorbing the last blood of the sunset. Reggie had told me that the ones with snow peaks were the head of the Spiti Valley. I could just make them out, but now they seemed very far away.

Spiti will change. Nothing can stop that. The people of the valley have a right to want the things that they believe will make their lives better, a television, an electric toothbrush, RayBan Aviator sunglasses. What threatens Spiti is that with the relaxation of border restrictions, the younger generation has the opportunity to leave the valley and head for the false god of the cities. Perhaps their altitude and isolation will protect them a little longer from what is inevitable, but the onus is really on those visitors who want to go in and see. Time-warped pockets always suffer when the gobbling dollar becomes the new currency, but it is up to the carrier of the dollars to decide the most regenerative method of spending the tourist buck.

Our little group may remember Spiti as we found it, in the same way that Reggie remembers the sweetness of Mrs Montagu's voice; they both have a rose-tinted hue. The ochre monks have survived this far with just the addition of a few digital watches and solar heating. Tabo may well enter the next millennium in a higher state of grace than the rest of us and on into the one after that. As long as there is the common bond that neither the young novice monks nor I understand the books of Julian Barnes, we may all perhaps progress together.

BIBLIOGRAPHY

BANCROFT, ANNE, *Religions of the East*, Heinemann 1974
BATCHELOR, STEPHEN, *The Tibet Guide*, Wisdom Publications 1987
CONZE, EDWARD, *A Short History of Buddhism*, Allen & Unwin 1980
HOPKIRK, PETER, *Trespassers on the Roof of the World*, Oxford University Press 1991
HUMPHREYS, CHRISTMAS, *A Popular History of Buddhism*, Curzon Press 1984
INSIGHT GUIDES, *India's Western Himalaya*, APA Publications 1992
KIPLING, RUDYARD, *Kim*, Penguin Books 1991
KUSY, FRANK, *Cadogan Guides India*, Cadogan Books 1992
LAMA, DALAI, *Freedom in Exile*, Hodder and Stoughton 1990
LION HANDBOOKS, *The World's Religions*, Lion Handbooks 1982
LONELY PLANET, *Trekking in the Indian Himalaya*, Lonely Planet 1986
NOBLE, CHRISTINA, *Over the High Passes*, Collins 1987
PADMASAMBHAVA, *The Tibetan Book of the Dead* translated by Robert A. F. Thurman, The Aquarius Press 1994
POWELL, ANDREW, *Living Buddhism*, British Museum Publications 1989
SWIFT, HUGH, *Trekking in India and Pakistan*, Hodder & Stoughton 1990
KINGDON WARD, FRANK, *The Land of the Blue Poppy*, Cadogan Books 1986